THRIVING JOURNEY OF ADOLESCENCE

SUKHMANPREET KAUR

To my wonderful parents and mamus,

Alongside with my **parents**, my **mamus** (maternal uncles) have been my greatest support in encouraging me to nurture my habit of journaling, which became a meaningful way to express myself. Support is vacant without blessings, and I am deeply grateful to my **Nani ji** (maternal grandmother) for her immense blessings.

Your unwavering faith and motivation have made this journey possible, enabling me to pursue my passion and share my words with the world.

Contents

Preface

The book delves into the complex world of teenagers, exploring the challenges they face as they navigate the path of self-discovery. It offers guidance on how teens can understand their own worth, find their voice, and embrace their uniqueness. Through this journey, many will encounter inner conflicts between their beliefs and actions—which can lead to confusion and self-doubt. The book also examines why relationship with parents often become strained during these years and how to manage these emotional shifts. By understanding themselves and their evolving identities, teens can foster healthier relationship with parents and develop the confidence to lead authentic lives. Living your life in pursuit of instant gratification, which lasts even for a short time, is not the true way to live your life to the fullest. To enjoy your life to the fullest, you need to step out of the sheltered boundaries of your comfort zone and reprogram your thinking the way you perceive the things. The book reflects how solipsistic thinking hinders personal growth. It aims not just to encourage you to survive through your teen years, but to embrace the idea of truly living—enjoy every moment of your life, rather than getting afraid of challenges.

Adore life and enjoy reading.

CHAPTER I

Teenage and Teenager

Our life learnings begin right when we are born. A child goes through multiple phases in their life. Throughout our life span, we go through different life stages which are likely to be like this:

Infant→ Child→ Teenager→ Adult→ Elder/retired person

The entire life-span is a learning period. Even an infant grasps expressions. An elderly person assimilates things. Grasping expressions from the surroundings is a lesson for an infant or child. The way to deal with vicissitudes is a lesson for a teenager or for an adult. Everyone is engaged in their own life lessons. The journey from our birth to death is all about learning, experiencing different contingencies, contending various vicissitudes. Each life stage teaches us valuable lessons. The learning of an infant includes the baby steps they take. It also includes crawling, grasping expressions from surroundings. The child stage, which is the next stage after infancy, includes walking, running and learning their native language. The crucial stage considered in every person's life is the Teenage or Adolescent stage. The Adult stage is considered the "Working stage." The next stage is considered as the retirement stage.

We are going to take a deep dive into the Teenage stage. This stage of life is considered "one of the most crucial stage." Although every stage of life is a consequential learning period. Nevertheless, this stage of life is more likely to be a CHANGING STAGE. "What is the reason for calling this stage a Changing Stage?"

This time period of life is a stage where physical, mental, emotional, cognitive changes, conscious and subconscious changes occur. This time period is strenuous to understand for every Teenager. Because even a scholar child seems to turn into an ignoramus child in this stage. If a teenager is able to understand what changes can occur and discovers ways to deal with them, they can sail through this stage effectively. It is not accurate to say it is easy, as no one can navigate through this stage effortlessly. Before diving deeper into the question of why this stage is called a changing stage. We need to look at the terms of Teenage and Teenagers.

Teenage- The life stage from age 13 to 19 is usually considered teenage. However, the life stage from the age of 10 to 20 is also considered *teenage*. Officially, an individual is considered an adult after 18; nevertheless, they may still exhibit emotions typical of a teenager, even at the age of 20.

Teenager- The person who is experiencing the teenage stage, is considered the teenager.

After the childhood phase, an individual enters a period of life where physical and mental changes occur in the body which is known as the teenage years. The stage is somewhat fluctuating and strenuous for many teenagers. The variations are hard to navigate. The vicissitudes which an individual has to confront are so different, as they seem.

Which are the arduous variations to manage?

- **PHYSICAL CHANGES** – At this stage, an individual's body experiences various biological changes.

- **EMOTIONAL CHANGES** – Due to physical changes, emotional states also fluctuate. Emotions vary rapidly and teenagers experience precipitous emotional surge. Overly emotional and easily getting thrilled are frequent signs of being a teenager.

All the variations that keep on happening, are the reason we call it a "CHANGING STAGE."

The changing stage is faced by teenagers during their teenage years. We believe a person has immense potential based on their age group, gender, economic and social status; however, regardless of any differences every person can accomplish any goal. However, no one realizes their potential instantly because it is a gradual process. When a person perceives, it gives an instant assuredness. We will be discerning about the teenagers' concerns and potential.

Teenagers' views of the world

HOW THE WORLD LOOKS LIKE TO A TEEANGER:
As long as a child remains just a child, their experiences are limited to observing the world. They observe the world in their own way (for instance, a child learning a language by observation), "regardless of thinking about 'WWWH,' which basically stands for What, When, Why and How."
Why things happen, How they happen, What happens, and when it happens, a child does not get affected by these thoughts.
Both infants and children observe the things happening around them; however, they look at them effortlessly, or we could say, superficially. Nevertheless, there are many incidents, which effect them mournfully. But they continue to observe and strive to experience more and more. As they grow, they feel they are improving themselves. As children grow up, they try to look at the world more deeply, and that is when adolescence begins to reflect in their behaviour. The view of the world for a teenager is a unique blend of curiosity, exploration, and evolving perspectives.
Teenagers step out of the sheltered boundaries of childhood. Teenagers become eager to explore different cultures, beliefs, and experiences. They approach the world with an open mind, embracing diversity and seeking opportunities to learn from distinct viewpoints.
When teenagers step up, they ponder about flying in the broad sky with their shrouded wings. The wings may appear somewhat hazy to others; nevertheless, those who want to feel, observe and have the aspiration to experience the world with vibrant colours, they try to fly. Those teenagers do not look after the things that pose resistance for them. The one thought they always pursue is that they are amateurs and want to become proficient in everything. And the words, "Proficient in everything" insist them to upscale.

WHAT TEENAGER DESIRES:

- They want to pursue what they desire.
- They want to get familiar with the world.
- They want to live a free and joking life.
- They want to be fathomless.
- Teenagers want to live their lives based on their own terms, with their own rules and conditions.

CHAPTER II

Pseudo truth at the age of 20

Before turning 20, a teenager has multiple thoughts. These thoughts vary; they could be about career, studies, finances, or life. They feel like they have to accomplish everything in a single attempt. At the moment when a teenager's life cycle begins, two thoughts arise:

1. **PSEUDO LUXURY IS REALITY:** The lavish life I have now is the reality; life is all about enjoying the luxuries using my parents' money. This thought process of enjoying luxuries from parents' money comes in two ways:

a) when teenagers get everything, whatever they want without muddling.

b) Peer pressure or the need to showcase themselves to society. While it is not the teenager's fault for being an overly showcasing person, but they are somehow affected by it.

2. **THE OUTER LUXURY IS NOT CONSTANT:** Some people think that the external showcase of extravagance is all pseudo; they know what the reality of life looks like. Those who understand that outer luxuries are not constant, going through ups and downs is the reality. They will not become depressed over and over again as they will be aware about the reality and they will live an authentic life.

On the other hand, for those who believe in the first thought, it is strenuous for them to trust in the reality of what life actually is! On the basis of their mindset, Teenagers can be categorized in the above two categories. The way they think about their life is all dependent on their belief. Based on their belief they believe in some pseudo truths as well which are:

- I will be happier if I have more friends.
- If I am not perfect at something, I am a failure.
- Self-growth can only be defined by popularity.
- Everything must be flawless and effortless.

- To live a successful life, I have to earn more.
- The more material things I have, the happier I will be.
- Failure defines that I am not good at anything.
- *My identity can only be determined by the number of people know me.*
- *My worth depends on the number of people like me.*
- Everyone seems to live a happier life except for me.
- I cannot resist procrastination.
- I cannot surpass my limits.
- It is too late to start anything new.
- In my opinion, life is stagnant and inconsistent.
- Happiness can only be attained through materialistic things.
- I can achieve anything by manifesting.
- It is essential to adopt all qualities to become a perfect person.
- To be successful, I have to be perfect.
- There is a need to avoid taking risks at all cost.
- Dreams are easily attainable.
- Consistency does not mean a lot.
- Everyone can be deemed trustworthy.
- It is not possible to alter the current situations.
- **There is a need to follow the same path my ideal took to achieve their goals.**
- Habits do not matter on the path to success.
- My current habits are inconsequential.
- Physical appearance always matters!
- There is a need to compare myself negatively to know my worth.*
- Dreams are devoid of realism.
- I must attain the peak of perfectionism in everything.
- It is not feasible to learn from failures.
- Endeavours harden the path and diminish my strength.
- The purpose of life is only to amass wealth.
- It is essential to refrain from engaging in the analytical process for any predicament.
- I ought to disclose my imperfections to all.

- I cannot withstand the repercussions.

    → The possible repercussions in a teenager's life could include lower academic achievement or losing in the sports competitions. These ramifications can only be possible if you would not be well prepared for your exams or adequately practiced for games. Therefore, it is illogical to assert that repercussions are irresistible.
- Intangible things do not possess substantial significance in real life.
- Disdaining the woes is the key to get rid of them.
- Everything [entire life] must be meticulously planned right now.
- The right time will come soon.

    → It is always the right time to engage in productive actions, such as studying; however, for a teenager, that right time never comes.
- Euphoria is constant.
- I'm too young to make a meaningful impact on the world.
- The grass is always greener on the other side.
- Others have favorable opportunities.
- I am devoid of opportunities.
- Our life is shaped by what we manifest.
- Everything will be sorted out through our manifestation.
- Everyone is an attentive listener.
- There is a need to showcase everything every time.

*Comparisons are of two types- Positive and Negative comparisons. You can read more about Comparisons from author's 1st book- "Bond with Reality of Life"

CHAPTER III

Truth at the age of 20

When a teenager moves from teenage and puts himself in the zone of adulthood, the perspectives of looking after everything changes. Majorly the perspectives are formed by listening from the surroundings. What the teenager observes from the community in his adulthood, it analyses the notions and make an overview of everything and realizes what one was doing. The major realization which mainly visible in majority is that: they realize what we were doing, or what they were thinking till the age of 20, those notions were all pseudo. Although everyman has disparate view over this, but truth is, it is hard to believe what is legitimate. In reality or simple words, the age of 20 can be considered as the "age of realization."

There are some truths which are usually considered true but some of them are considered as Pseudo.

Knowing what is the reality, it takes years to realize.

The major hardship is recognition of legitimate and misleading thoughts. What we see is not real every time, what we hear is not true each time.

There are some major truths which must be known to every teen are:

- Your whole odyssey is self-discovery.
- You need to overcome self-sabotaging.
  [Here, self-sabotage resembles ensnarements such as procrastination, substance abuse and social media obsession.]
- You have more resilience than you think.
- You already have a lot on your plate; you shouldn't feel obligated to address every single issue.
- You do not have to be overwhelmed all the time.

- To learn from experiences, be a documentarian. Wrap your life moments in a diary to learn from the past in the future.
- The definition of success varies for everyone; there is not a well-defined definition.
- An authentic amicability bond exists only with parents.
- Success can't be confined to 2-3 words.
- Debacles bestow us the opportunity of learning and growing.
- Failures guide us on how to be acme.
- Nothing remains stagnant.
  If something is stagnant, then there are two possibilities:

  - Either you are putting your whole efforts or not.
  - God has orchestrated something better for you.

- The pragmatism is antithetical to dream life.
- Day dreaming never proclaims the prevalence of life.
- Mental health and Physical health must be accentuated.
- One should assimilate the art of balancing.
- For personal growth, it is a must to elude the comfort sphere.
- Distinctiveness is the real identity of everyone and each person has their unique strengths and weaknesses.
- Mastering the art of conversational eloquence is a must.
- The investment you make on yourself it will yield better rewards that are unmeasurable.
- Learn the artifice of team-work.
- Treat others as you want to be treated.
- Making mistakes is usual; there is no need to feel degraded.
- One should embrace the change and practice gratitude.
- The exact meaning of independence is being responsible for your actions.
- There is nothing wrong with following your passion and hobbies that bring you joy.
- Feedback is the key to learning from your flaws!
- It is okay to be authentic instead of trying to be fit into a perturbed zone.

- Money management skills are crucial for financial stability.
- Listening to disparate perspectives is helpful in broadening your horizons.
- It's okay to say "no" to things that don't align with your values.
- Building a supportive network is preeminent for personal development.
- Family plays an eloquent role in shaping our personality.
- Appreciate the life blessings.
- Embrace every change as an opportunity for learning and growing.
- Faith in God helps you to follow the right path and feel satisfied.
- To understand others better, empathy and understanding are essential.
- It is okay to take pauses (small breaks).
- It's okay to seek professional help for mental health concerns.
- Curiosity always helps in learning new things!
- Growing gradually is prosaic; nevertheless, it is efficacious.
- Accepting yourself as you are.
- Nothing good happens if you consistently degrade yourself.
- You will feel scared and emotional, and that is okay because, after all, you are human. You might feel horrible about your future, and these emotions may even make you feel suffocated. It is alright to snivel, but you don't need to express these emotions in front of others. Instead, **express them to yourself**—that is the true way to manage and control your emotions.

The life of a teenager is the composition of experiencing every emotion, including hard times and enjoyable moments. Hard periods can bring dreadful times, anxiety, stress, mournful days or even it can be felt that life will remain the same forever. Sometimes, the level of ecstasy is alacritous but remember, opportunities arise; sometimes it is about either facing and accepting failures, or cherishing accomplishments. The life stage of a teenager, is full of uncertainties. The people who overcome many failures are the ones who truly succeed in their teenage years. Achieving success from teenage is a long pursuit that every individual desires; however, not every person has potential to attain it. It is the time when some people make mistakes that can affect them for the rest of their lives, while others build a firm foundation for their future. Envision yourself as the person you want to be in the future and keep that image clearly in your mind so as not to get distracted by unwanted desires. Entrench some principles for yourself to be consistent and focused on your goals. Deliberate and discuss your notions with yourself repeatedly to be legitimate with your thoughts and track your progress. If you truly want to remain authentic be aligned with your principles. Your principles and the manifested version of yourself will shape your character, and it will be advantageous in guiding you to take actions that align with your short-term and long-term aspirations.

Your inner self and outer expressions will align with your actions because, at your core, you are aligned with your principles and the manifested version of yourself. Your principles and manifested version involve establishing distinct boundaries, nurturing your habits conducive to productivity, and embracing resilience when confronted with challenges. **_Another reality is that you can become a better version of yourself—just be honest with yourself._**

CHAPTER IV

Plasticity

4.1 INTRODUCTION

As we grow and evolve over time, our brain develops, our notions and thoughts grow. As we grow over time, we get influenced by distinct factors. The factors might be affecting us directly or indirectly, cause sudden alteration or gradual change, ubiquitous disruption or limited constancy. Whenever a child listens to a story or thought, the child tries to adapt to the situation. The children try to consume more and more information, and as they consume the information about distinct topics, their brains become adaptable to the situation. If a person is learning coding and coding coherently, there are greater chances that the person will be able to code in lesser time. That is the *concept of adaptability. Teenagers* do not realize that they are experiencing plasticity—their brain's ability to adapt, grow, and rewire itself as they are consuming new information and challenging themselves. Every coding attempt, every solved problem, and every failure they learn to strengthens their ability to think reasonably and creatively. The more they consume, the more they adapt and this notion, which makes the brain more adaptable, is referred to as Plasticity. *In the context of teenagers, plasticity or neuroplasticity refers to alteration, adaptation and responding to the environment.*

4.2 ROLE OF PLASTICITY IN TEENAGERS' LIFE

The way we mold clay, it takes the shape of that mold. Similarly, during the time period from childhood to adolescence, notions affect teenagers' brains. A brain is adaptable; the kinds of thoughts brain process it tries to mold it into that form. In the context of neuroscience, plasticity refers to the brain's ability to reorganize itself by forming new neural connections. Although, it is not true that neural connections are built only during adolescence. New neural connections are formed at every stage of life, but the thoughts developed during this period immensely impact a teenager's mind. Any traumatic incident that happens during adolescence can have lasting impacts even later in life. Due to greater chances of impacts, it is necessary to implicate more positive changes and indulge a teenage in the positive environment. The role of plasticity in teenagers' lives is multifaceted which impacts various aspects of their cognitive, emotional, and social well-being.

4.3 ROLE IN BRAIN DEVELOPMENT

Neuroplasticity, or simply plasticity, is a **fundamental property of the brain that refers to its ability to reorganize itself by forming new neural connections throughout life.** This process is prominent in the development of the brain. There are some key aspects of role of plasticity in brain's development:

- Learning: When burgeoning youth are exposed to learning, the brain's ability increases to form new neural connections, and synaptic connections are also strengthened to retain knowledge for a longer time. Neuroplasticity helps the brains of teenagers to forge and strengthen connections so they can remember and practically use what they have learned.
- Resilience: A blossoming teen is more conscious about adapting their own thoughts, and plasticity **allows a teen to think flexibly.** Due to resilient feature of neuroplasticity, they *adapt their thoughts* and perform actions according to different circumstances and this proves to be significant for problem-solving, decision-making, and overall brain functioning.
- Equanimity: A psychological state of being calm. To be mindfulness, plasticity offers teenagers the feature of equanimity, as they can adapt, handle and *reorganize themselves according to the demands of the environment* or during any social, emotional or physical change.
- Managing: Neuroplasticity helps in developing self-awareness, empathy and handling hysterical situations.

  A burgeoning teen's brain changes how it processes emotional

and social transformations. With the development of emotions like self-awareness and empathy, their brain develops the ability to comprehend and deal with social circumstances. In simpler words:

As a teenager's brain develops, it learns to handle social situations better. The brain changes the way it processes emotions and social experiences, which help the teenagers understand and respond to those situations more effectively.

- Synaptic Pruning: It is a natural process that occurs in the brain between early childhood and adolescence. Under this process, the extra synapses get eliminated, as a teen grows older and learns new complex information, the brain becomes more efficient by removing connections that are no longer needed. This process is essential for maintaining optimal brain function.

Neuroplasticity holds a pivotal aspect in brain development; however, development of teen's brain is an unceasing process that helps in decision-making, and long-term planning.

4.4 HOW DOES PLASTICITY GETS AFFECTED?

We all get greatly impacted by our surroundings and the environment we live in. In the place we live, we adapt the habits and the characteristics of that environment. Both knowingly and unknowingly, we can feel influenced by the environment. *Our thoughts and notions are* immensely *impacted by* our *environment and as well as by the media* which is elaborated below:

- Experience dependent plasticity: The experiences of a person's life do matter a lot to every individual. The kind of environment a child is surrounded by, it is not wrong to say that a child will be of that nature. In some areas, it is often seen, if any family member is scurrilous in nature, it would effect the soundness of mind of a child. And, it is more obvious, a child would adapt to that kind of nature as well. Unless a teen is treated morally well, it is obvious, a teen would not be able to make him/her self morally persistent.

- Media Exposure: Nowadays, teenagers are more exposed to the media. They are more attracted towards screens; screen time is increasing day-by-day. Not only in teenage, but also in other stages of life, exorbitant usage of social media and watching inappropriate content unremittingly, will lead to pessimistic effects on the moral values of a teenager. Teenage is the time period when a teen grows morally and socially. Social media provides platforms to showcase skills. However, with the positive impacts, there is another side of the coin as well which would be negative. Social media exposes a teen to the global world at an early stage, which has partially positive and partially negative impacts. At an early age chit-chatting with unidentified people, might not be prolific.

4.5 IMPACTS OF NEUROPLASTICITY

As we got to know how neuroplasticity gets impacted by the environment and media, now we need to know, how it impacts our thought process positively and negatively. What are the changes that can be brought about through neuroplasticity? Neuroplasticity can bring either positive or negative alterations.

Constructive Outcomes:

- Vanquish Psychiatric Problems: In a non-stop hustle life, nowadays, people might be suffering from some mental disorders. Cognitive-behavioural therapy (CBT), Dialectical Behavioural Therapy (DBT), Family Counselling and therapies help people to reframe their negative thought patterns. When a person habitually practices a new and affirmative way of thinking, certainly, it can rewire the brain's response to stress and improve their mental health. As neuroplasticity is about bringing alterations and adapting, so once an individual will brings positive change and adapts it, neuroplasticity underlies the brain's ability to adopt these healthier thinking patterns.
- Competence: During adolescence, the human brain is adept at forming new synaptic connections, which enables teenagers to

learn new skills and retain information more effectively.

- Cognitive Reappraisal: It refers to changing the way one thinks about a situation in order to alter its emotional impact. As teenagers experience various emotions, the ability of Cognitive Reappraisal helps them to rewire their thinking. Their brain will form and strengthen neural pathways. The stronger Cognitive Reappraisal, teenagers will have a more enhanced ability to think about a situation in a different way, which will help them to have more strong emotional regulation.

Detrimental Outcomes:

- Susceptibility to Negative Influences: Due to neuroplasticity, a teen's brain is highly adaptable, it is susceptible that under the influence of negative surroundings, a teen will engage in some malevolent practices such as substance abuse. Negative surroundings can include peer pressure or negative role models. They could be influencers. It does not mean that every influencer has a negative influence. The issue is that when a teen begins to relate their life to that of an influencer, they always want that every aspect of their life must be relatable. To some extent it is beneficial; however, excessive exposure is always toxic. Consuming or doing anything in excess can be harmful.
- Impact of Technology: As the brain is adaptive to alterations, technology impacts a teen in various aspects:
  1. Disrupted sleeping cycle
  2. Time management
  3. Impact on the eyes
  4. Cyberbullying
  5. Privacy invasion
  6. Body image issues
  7. Hindrance in Personal Development
  8. Apprehension

These consequences might sound general; however, the results will be disastrous, and over the long term, the consequences will be even more catastrophic.

- Emotional Volatility: A teen's brain is in a state of rapid development. which makes it more sensitive to emotional stimuli. The human brain is highly responsive to stress. Chronic stress during this period can lead to maladaptive changes in the brain's structure and function, increasing the risk of anxiety disorders. Due to perturbation (A situation that affects the usual state of emotions, leading to sudden changes) mood swings can occur, making it complicated for teenagers to superintend their emotions efficaciously.

Limitation:

One of the key limitation of the neuroplasticity is, *it declines with age.* Over the years, as the body becomes less flexible, so does the brain. A significant amount of neuroplasticity is focused on helping young people comprehend and interact with their environment. So, as it lasts for limited period, it is like an evanescent gem.

Apparently, it is up to the teenager **what sort of impact of neuroplasticity, one wants to implement in their life?**

Options: A (Constructive Outcomes) or B (Detrimental Outcomes)

Your Answer: ______

CHAPTER V

Ephemeral Gratification

6.1 INTRODUCTION

Party Spree: Alex and his buddies decided to spend their weekend in Las Vegas. They went there to enjoy a trip. They thought it would be a trip to remember which would be filled with gambling, parties, and fun. However, when Tom returned home, he felt an unexpected emptiness. He had a good time there with his buddies; however, he was not feeling satisfied. He also had a big bill to pay. This made Alex think about planning his next holidays differently, looking for trips that would give him real joy rather than just quick excitement. The Social Media Buzz: In the realm of social media, Emily shared a snapshot of her vacation. Rapidly, the likes and comments cascaded like a waterfall. The initial likes surged through her veins, filling her with excitement. But as the notifications dwindled, so did her elation. A hunger for more likes and comments gnawed at her, which reveals ephemeral gratification.

The above examples highlight that the actions which give impulsive reactions do not last for a longer time. There is an emotion of instant exhilaration. This intense elation can provide a brief moment of pleasure but often leaves a lasting sense of emptiness or regret in the long term. But now, some questions arise: What is Ephemeral Gratification? What factors affect it? What are its consequences? From the above examples, Ephemeral Gratification can be defined as the instant elation for shorter time, which does not have a long-lasting effect. It is the desire for and the experience of **immediate pleasure** without any delay. In modern times, due to advancement in technology and even due to cultural shifts, ephemeral gratification has became so prevalent. It acts as an instantaneous reward but without long-term rewards. There are few characteristics of ephemeral gratification which are given below:

6.2 CHARACTERISTICS

1. Immediacy: The speed at which a reward can be received is instant. Its range even lies in between from seconds to minutes. As seen in example 2, the social buzz does not remain for a longer time. As the notifications slowed down, so did the elation. It is akin to a loophole in which teenagers strive for likes and comments but in the end, they feel empty and isolated. Practically getting likes on personal accounts does not matter, however, for a professional account, it does matter because there you have to show your work. People work nisusly (mentally and physically) to attain followers which affect functioning of human brain.

2. Satisfaction: This process involves the ease of receiving instant reward, so satisfaction looks glorious and immense. Although, it lacks long-term fulfilment. The constant pursuit of these short-term pleasures can hinder a teenager from pursuing more meaningful activities such as personal achievements or personal growth. Patience and resilience start fading away in teenagers' life. Long-term goal setting can be delayed due to ephemeral gratification, which is not favourable for long term success and well-being of a teenager.

3. Ease of Access: In the digital age, ephemeral gratification is ubiquitous, people of all ages can access the internet which is full of deception. A coin has always two sides, nevertheless, social media is merely illusory. It resists teenagers to look after the other side of the coin. The moment a teenager becomes familiar with social media, it becomes addictive to it. The primary concern is that personal validation has been demolished. A teenager gets validation through likes and comments especially from their unidentified friends. Even peer pressure cannot be neglected; under that pressure teenagers use the social media. Under peer pressure, teenagers feel the marathon of attaining followers. The issues like body image, substance abuse became substantial predicaments. Peer pressure can be covered extensively.

The features have been covered, now the question is, what are the factors affecting ephemeral gratification?

6.3 FACTORS AFFECTING

In this digital age, teenagers feel instant gratification through multiple factors such as:

- Social Media
- Instant Messaging Applications
- Streaming platforms
- Mobile and Computer games
- Viral Socializing Applications
- Online Trends
- Online Shopping
- Music Streaming that caters your every preference according to your choice.

All these factors promptly incite and fluster a teenager. The allure of digital media lies in their content which connects a teenager to the real-time and its ability to offer real time social interactions. It even has the ability to provide the instant validation through the features of their applications, which can become compulsive in the long-run. Quick rewards and levels in the games keep players hooked and teenagers develop obsessive focus in instantaneous gratification. This kind of mania is detrimental. As earlier said, teenagers face perturbations with regards to their mental health, so the access to colossal libraries of these platforms work for them as escapism. Scientifically studies have verified that digital media platforms leads to superfluous release of Dopamine which is a relaxing hormone. *Peer pressure and Soundness of mind of teenagers are the key sources of hook for these platforms; due to these factors teenagers get captivated to digital platforms.* The constant accessibility of friends and the ease of communication keep teenagers engaged. The convenience of online shopping provides a quick thrill and the anticipation of package arrival.

6.4 CONSEQUENCES

"In the endeavour of chasing short term nostalgia, we obliviate to grasp real cherishment in life."

Ephemeral gratification is the pursuit of immediate relish, so, it is obvious that, it will come with range of consequences, which can be either positive or negative.

Positive Impact-

- During disquietude, ephemeral gratification can act as escapism.
- It can help in devastating affliction.
- Participating in activities that provide immediate satisfaction can be a way to celebrate small victories and boost motivation for tackling larger tasks.

Negative Impacts-

"Short-term pleasure leads to long-term regret."

- It resists the self-discipline and persistence of a teenager.
- A teenager's ability to be resilient begins to diminish.
- Self-Governance: The immediate desire to get something can weaken one's self-control and in the long run, a teen will be immensely impacted by this habit of instant gratification. The ability to control one's desire will be diminished and it can even the weaken the ability to practice delayed gratification. For instance:
A teen needs a gaming PC and feels immense glee at that thought. In that case, a teen will not have the ability to control himself. He might insist on getting the PC immediately. This is because his ability of controlling himself in the delayed gratification has been diminished.
- Financial Instability: The proclivity for impulsive spending driven by the desire for instant glee can lead to financial

instabilities. Habit of saving for future extenuate.

- Reduce Satisfaction: Over time, instant pleasure reduces the satisfaction, which leads to emptiness. Truly meaningful sources of happiness are often neglected.

6.5 HOW IT RESIST IN GROWTH

William, a high school student, often plays video games instead of studying for exams.

Dopamine Release: Playing video games releases *dopamine* in William's brain, which creates pleasure and reward. This immediate gratification reinforces his gaming habit over studying.

Impact: While gaming, William's body becomes less active for planning and controlling his impulses. This hinders his ability to prioritize long-term goals like studying.

Consequence: William will glorify the immediate pleasure of gaming and undervalue the future benefits of good grades. This leads to repeated short-term gratification, negatively affecting his academic performance and personal growth.

The pursuit of instant glee leads to reduced self-control, resulting in poor decision-making. This behaviour becomes the cause of neglecting long-term goals, stagnated personal development and leading to reduced life satisfaction.

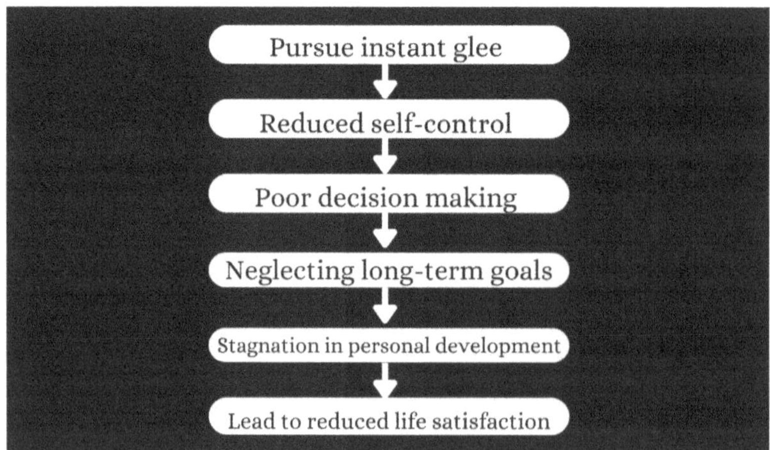

Ephemeral Gratification

"Sacrificing future growth for present comfort is a pessimistic trade that stagnant personal development."

Apparently, it is up to the teenager what sort of pleasure one wants? **Either short term or long term.**
Before deciding do not obliviate that-
Ephemeral gratification is the enemy of sustained success and lifelong satisfaction.

• • •

Action-Plan: 2-Minute Reflection and Action rule by Sukhmanpreet Kaur
To resist yourself, you can follow this 2-minute reflection and action. Whenever you feel like doing something for ephemeral gratification, take 2 minutes to reflect on your long-term goals of the week. This is reflection. Then assign yourself a journalling task. During journalling, write what you planned to watch or do. And at the end, write the negative consequences of watching. This is Action. Your mind will automatically resist you to perform the task which is affecting you negatively. Earlier, no one was resisting you, but now, you have written yourself, that this is the negative consequence of scrolling. The time has been gone, so, it is hard to go back to that and also your impulse to get instant glee has been reduced.

CHAPTER VI

Management (Quotes)

"If you are unable to manage great things, then manage small things in a great way, and they will eventually turn out great."

"Refrain managing your time—take actions based on the time you have, because tomorrow right at this time, you will say, 'I wish I had started yesterday.'"

"We delay taking actions on time, but time will not delay in passing by."

"We delay taking actions on time, but time will not delay in passing by."

CHAPTER VII

Ostensible Behaviour

7.1 INTRODUCTION

The word Ostensible means 'to show.' It refers to behaviour or actions of presenting an outward appearance that may differ from one's inner reality. In today's fast-paced world, ostensible behaviour often involves presenting a facade to meet social norms, expectations, or to gain acceptance in society while hiding one's true feelings, thoughts, or intentions. Teenagers often strive to maintain a standardized social norm which has been set by society. The concept of the "persona," aligns closely with ostensible behaviour. Persona can be defined as the social face an individual presents to the world. It is a kind of mask teenagers design to make a particular impression on others.

Ostensible behaviour is closely intertwined with the concepts of persona and lowest point. Persona refers to the feign social face an individual presents to the world. A teen embodies multifaceted experiences including emotional, social, and psychological challenges. These challenges are seen as the lowest point during adolescence. The consequence of lowest point is that it can leave teenagers with overwhelmed emotions and feeling isolated. When teenagers try to overcome the situations, but they are unable to tackle them due to lack of guidance, teenagers feel at their lowest in that moment. Teenagers don't express their true emotions to trusted individuals, that is where behaviour of persona reflects in their character. This is how the ostensible behaviour is meticulously intertwined with the persona and the lowest point. The consequences will be explained further.

Fitting In: Emma, a high school student, was known for her enthralling personality. She was always the centre of attention at social gatherings and school events. However, her close friends knew that Emma was struggling with feelings of vacillation and self-doubt. She used to mask her internal struggles to fit within her peers.

Workplace Dynamics: Oliver, a young professional, incessantly attended after-work social events and always seemed enthusiastic about team activities. However, in reality, Oliver was introverted and preferred spending time alone or with close friends. Still, he engaged in activities to fit in, with his colleagues and avoid being seen as antisocial, fearing it might affect his career prospects.

These two examples indicate the inclusion of individuals in the ostensible behaviour. Their ostensible behaviour acted as a mask which hid their vulnerabilities to meet social expectations.

> "*To be yourself and standing out as different is the ultimate achievement in a world where everyone tries to fit you into societal norms.*"

7.2 HOW LOWEST POINT HIT?

Teenage is the age of exploration, where teenagers begin the process of becoming conscious of themselves whether through physical development, career exploration, or social inclusion. When teenagers step out to world exploration in search of meaningful knowledge, they encounter the multifaceted world. Certain norms are already set which everyone has to follow to fit into meretricious groups of peers that are attractive in a flashy way but lack true worth or have no real worth such as, a teenager can't be considered 'cool' unless they engage in substance use. Out of fear of social exclusion, a teen may take specific actions to fit into peers' group. Societal inclusion becomes essential for the teenager. When teenagers are trapped in the loophole of trying to fit in, it becomes resistance for them in growing, focusing on personal development and interpersonal skills. When teenagers are without guidance, they keep falling into the loophole, which becomes strenuous for teenagers to step out of the trap. Interpersonal skills and guidance are necessary for each teenager. If they do not have someone authentic with whom they can share their emotions, they will surely begin to feel isolated. And also, if teenagers are not admirers of self-talk (a part of interpersonal skills) they will conflict with their own thoughts. It is often seen that teenagers feel hesitant to share their emotions with their parents. This avoidance becomes the cause of the situation becoming critical, and this is how teenagers have to confront the lowest point in their lives.

A Silent Struggle: At 17, Laura moved to a new school in the middle of her sophomore year which had turned her life upside down. Desperate to fit in, she tried everything: new clothes, a different hairstyle, even a change in attitude. But nothing seemed to work for her. The popular kids of the school ignored her, and the ones she wanted to be friends with seemed to have their own peers already. Feeling increasingly isolated, Laura kept her struggles to herself. She did not want to burden her parents, who were already stressed about the move and their new jobs. Every day, she plastered on a smile before heading to school, but the loneliness gnawed at her. The situation reached its lowest point when her grades started to slip, and she withdrew further into herself, feeling like a stranger in her own home.

Laura chose ostensible behaviour and she fell into the trap of Lowest Point where she felt all alone. That is how every teenager experiences the loneliness due to various situations. But here, a question arises: what are the societal norms due to which a teen faces lowest point and has to choose ostensible behaviour!

7.3 SOCIETAL NORMS

Societal norms influence **behaviour, interactions, and self-perception** of teenagers. Usually, these norms are shaped by peer culture, media, and the broader social environment, and they can vary extensively across various groups and communities. There are some prevalent societal norms among teenagers:

1. *Physical appearance:* To fit among peers, generally there are three prerequisites:

- Impeccable- An individual has to be flawless. Physical appearance should be immaculate.
- Staying with current fashion trends is seen as a status symbol. It is seen as high value if a teen wears the latest styles and brands to gain acceptance and attain status among peers, although it is spurious.
- There is a strong emphasis on achieving a certain body type, influenced by their idol influencers, which can lead to pressure related to intense dieting, exercise routines, and physical enhancements.

2. *Social media presence:* Maintaining an engaging digital presence is essential. Teens judge each other on the basis of the number of likes, comments, and followers they get.

3. *Communication:* Using current slang and jargon is a way to fit in and to be part of the peer group. Staying updated with the latest terms is important for social integration.

4. *Resplendent image:* Unusual actions, such as substance abuse or partying are seen superior, but in reality, it is merely an ostentation.

5. *Independent:* There are certain boundaries which have been set by parents, but in an attempt to appear "lit" within the community, not obeying them is deceptively seen as independence. The true meaning of independence is achieving financial self-sufficiency; however, this definition has been distorted.

7.4 Factors AffectingOstensible Norms:

- Peer pressure
- Social media
- Unhealthy educational environment: An unhealthy school environment does not impact a teenager positively. An institution where unsound competition occurs, the emotion of spite and disdain at its peak, a teen will not flourish academically.
- Change in routine: Moving to a new city or changing schools impact teenagers. To avoid adopting ostensible behaviour,

changes can't be neglected. They are essential and one has to be mentally prepared for any kind of alteration in the environment.

Norms prevail in society, and if someone thinks of bursting all the misconceptions, remember a coin always has two sides. The norms are constant in nature. Therefore, it is up to teenagers to decide how they will deal with unusual circumstances and which norms they should follow that align with their values.

7.5 CONSEQUENCES OF OSTENSIBLE BEHAVIOUR

Individuals are not true to their authentic selves. To gain approval, or to avoid criticism, they ultimately undermine personal well-being and fulfilment. The consequences of this behaviour are multifaceted, impacting psychological health, academic as well as professional performance, and overall life satisfaction.

Few consequences of ostensible behaviour:

- Degrading their own worth.
- Social Isolation: Teenagers keep themselves isolated from social gatherings and interactions, which results in a lack of opportunities to build a professional network.
- Engaging in risky behaviour, such as substance abuse, to fit into peer groups and to overcome the stress caused by the fear of social exclusion.
- Due to lack of self-esteem, academic performance tends to be subpar.
- Due to insufficiency of self-awareness, an individual will struggle to understand their own personality traits, including strengths and weaknesses.
- There will be emotional distress.
- There are higher chances of missing professional opportunities due to emotional distress.
- You would live inauthentically.
- Because of inauthenticity, one could live a life filled with regrets.
- One will struggle to find the purpose of life, which will result in dissatisfaction with the decision- making process.

- Constantly hiding one's true self can lead to emotional exhaustion.
- Overall, this behaviour of teenagers affect their satisfaction and fulfilment in life.

7.6 SOLUTIONS

There can be multiple solutions to overcome this behaviour:

- Embracing authenticity.
- Fostering open communication with parents.
- Being mentally prepared for the changes.
- Practice Mindfulness through activities like meditation or breathing exercises to stay connected to your true self.
- Align with your values and morals.
- If nothing works out, it is perfectly okay to seek professional help if needed.

7.7 EMBRACING AUTHENTICITY

One should not try to conform to others' expectations. A teen should always embrace authenticity, which means being true to oneself. *Authenticity* refers to *self-actualization—where individuals strive to become their true selves and fulfil their potential—and being open to new experiences, accepting one's feelings and thoughts without denial or distortion.*

As in the above example of Laura, she tried to adopt ostensible behaviour, which did not work for her. On the other hand, if she had chosen to be herself only, she did not have to face the 'silence struggle.' Just by embracing her authenticity, she could have scored better in her exams. Even if other classmates ignored her, her skills and authenticity could have led her peers to appreciate her; however, she didn't choose wisely. Her decision-making wasn't wise.

If she had chosen to share with her parents, they could inspire her, guide her and help her to step out of the situation. **IT IS ESSENTIAL TO SHARE WITH PARENTS.** *Embrace your true self, for meaningful* *existence.*

Embracing Authenticity

At the end, teenagers have to decide for themselves what is best
for them:
a) Either a stressful life under ostensible behaviour
or
b) Blissful moments in life by praising themselves!

"Do not forget: if you exist, you do matter."

Now, answer this:
whether, A or B _______?

CHAPTER VIII

Conscientiousness

8.1 INTRODUCTION

Conscientiousness is the personality trait of being responsible, careful or diligent. It is about being disciplined, organized, and goal-oriented. It means taking tasks seriously and doing them to the best of one's ability and it is crucial as it influences the many aspects of a teen's life. Conscientiousness leads to create discipline in life which helps in self-growth. A conscientious person is independent in their thoughts. They keep their promises, meet deadlines, and fulfil their responsibilities. They are peculiar about their duties, for instance, they complete their homework on time, participate actively in group projects, and prepare thoroughly for exams. They understand the importance of planning ahead to complete their targets on **time.** It is clear that being conscientious means having a strong sense of self-discipline and avoiding the temptation of procrastination.

Conscientiousness encompasses qualities such as carefulness, the propensity to plan ahead and follow rules.

Balancing Work and School: Max works at a part-time job after school to help his family with expenses. Despite his busy schedule, he manages to keep up with his homework and participate in school clubs. He keeps a detailed planner to organize his tasks and sets aside specific times for studying, working, and relaxing. His conscientious nature ensures that he meets his responsibilities both at home and at school.

Time Management: Julia is involved in several school clubs and takes advanced placement courses. To manage her busy schedule, she creates a daily to-do list and prioritizes her tasks. She allocates specific time slots for studying, club meetings, and personal hobbies. Her conscientious time management skills help her excel in her academics and extracurricular activities without feeling overwhelmed.

"A teenager who embraces conscientiousness learns to bridge the gap from being a potential amateur to becoming a skilled and mature adult."

8.2 RELATION OF CONSCIENTIOUSNESS WITH CONFORMITY

Conformity

Conformity refers to the act of aligning one's attitudes, beliefs, and behaviours with those of a group or societal norms. To establish a social identity during adolescence, there is always a fear of rejection and desire for acceptance. To overcome the fear and in the desire for acceptance teens often conform to peer pressure, and societal norms.

Conscientiousness

Conscientious individuals are typically self-disciplined, goal-oriented, and mindful of their actions.

Conformity and conscientiousness are two distant yet interrelated concepts that can significantly influence teenagers' behaviours and development. Even if a teen is conscientious, still conformity and conscientiousness are inter-related. Here is how they are inter-related:

- Influence of Peer Pressure: Teenagers with high levels of conscientiousness may still conform to peer pressure, but their conformity is likely more selective and aligned with their values and goals. They might conform to positive behaviours, such as academic achievement or healthy lifestyle choices but at some point, they might conform to negative conformities such as:
Overdependence on external validation: A conscientious teen might conform to seeking approval from peers for their achievements, which can lead to an overreliance on external validation rather than internal satisfaction.**Avoidance of risks-taking:**While generally cautious, a conscientious teen might conform to a peer group's avoidance of healthy risk-taking, such

as not trying new activities or avoiding challenges due to fear of failure or judgment.

- Social Expectations: Conscientious teenagers are often more attuned to meeting social expectations. They may conform to societal norms that emphasize responsibility and academic success. Such teenagers might also experience *internal conflicts* if the group's expectations clash with their personal values and standards.

- Suppression of True Personality: Conforming to group norms that do not align with their conscientious nature can cause teenagers to suppress their true personality, leading to a lack of authenticity. Over time, this can result in decreased self-esteem or identity confusion. However, if a teen aligns with its morals, a teen will not feel disenfranchised (a feeling of being marginalized or deprived of one's own identity or rights within a group)

Understanding the relationship between conformity and conscientiousness can help parents, educators, and mentors to support teenagers in developing healthy and responsible behaviour,s. Encouraging positive peer associations and fostering environments that promote ethical standards. Moreover, supporting teenagers in their pursuit of personal goals can enhance their conscientiousness.

8.3 WAYS TO OVERCOME NEGATIVE CONFORMITY

- Foster Open Communication: Encourage teenagers to discuss their feelings and experiences with conformity and peer pressure.

- Promote Positive Role Models: Highlight individuals or groups that embody both high conscientiousness and positive conformity.

- Support Goal Setting: Help teenagers set and achieve personal goals, reinforcing the value of conscientiousness.

- Encourage Critical Thinking: Teach teenagers to critically evaluate the norms and behaviours they are conforming to and to make choices that align with their values.

8.4 BENEFITS OF CONSCIENTIOUSNESS

- Moral and Ethical Development: Conscientiousness is closely linked to moral and ethical behaviour. Teenagers with high conscientiousness are likely to conform to ethical standards and societal rules, avoiding behaviours they perceive as wrong or harmful. This alignment can guide their decisions, making them less likely to engage in activities like cheating, lying, or stealing, even if these behaviours are common among their peers.
- Academic and Extracurricular Activities: In academic settings, conscientious teenagers might conform to norms that favour hard work, punctuality, and adherence to rules and regulations. This can lead to higher academic performance and participation in structured extracurricular activities. Conformity in these areas can positively reinforce their conscientious traits, creating a cycle of achievement and self-discipline.
- Identity Formation: During adolescence, teenagers are in the process of forming their identities. Conscientious teenagers may be more deliberate in this process, choosing to conform to groups and activities that reflect their emerging sense of self. They are likely to seek out peers and mentors who support their goals and values, thereby reinforcing their conscientious behaviours.

8.5 CONSEQUENCES

While conscientiousness often leads to high levels of responsibility but it can also foster an excessive tendency towards negative conformity. Individuals who are highly conscientious may feel compelled to adhere strictly to rules, norms, and societal expectations, **even when these may not align with their personal values or beliefs.** This can stifle creativity and critical thinking, as the desire to be seen as reliable and diligent might overshadow the importance of independent thought and innovation. Consequently, conscientious individuals may find themselves prioritizing conformity over authenticity which would lead to stress, dissatisfaction, and a lack of fulfilment.

- Those with lower conscientiousness may be more susceptible to negative peer influences, potentially engaging in risky or irresponsible behaviours.
- Reduced Creativity and Innovation: High conscientiousness often involves a strong adherence to rules and norms. When paired with conformity, this can lead to hindrance in innovation and creativity.
- Overcommitment to Norms: Conscientious individuals may feel a strong obligation to conform to social norms, even if those norms are unethical, such as engaging in risky behaviour under the influence of peer pressure. If a social norm within a peer group encourages risky behaviours like underage drinking or substance abuse, a conscientious teenager might feel compelled to participate out of fear of exclusion and to be accepted by the group despite their personal discomfort.
- Loss of Individuality: The drive to conform can result in a loss of personal identity and individuality.
- Difficulty in Adaptation: While conscientiousness combined with conformity, this can result in resistance to change, making it difficult to adapt to new situations or environments.

8.6 CURTAIL YOUR ENERGETIC PERMEABILITY

Curtailing your energetic permeability means consciously reducing the extent to which you allow outside influences to affect your personal space and well-being. By doing so, you create a protective barrier around yourself. Curtailing your energetic permeability in relation to ethics and morals involves setting boundaries to protect your values and integrity from being compromised by external influences. By limiting how much you let others' behaviours or opinions affect you, you ensure that your personal principles remain intact. This practice helps you stay true to your own ethical standards and moral beliefs, even when faced with situations or people that might challenge or pressure you to compromise. It's a way of maintaining your moral compass and staying grounded in what you believe is right, regardless of external pressures. Setting boundaries is helpful for conscientious teens to overcome fear of negative conformity.

"Limit your boundaries to protect your moral, ethical values and your conscientiousness."

• • •

Key Takeaway: If you want to be an authentic conscientious individual, make sure to set your boundaries to avoid pursuing negative conformity.

CHAPTER IX

Paradigm

9.1 INTRODUCTION

Paradigm is the framework through which teenagers represent their unique world. Everyone has distinct experiences and a **unique thought process.** Paradigm is the way to think—how to pursue actions.

> "*We don't observe things based on how they are; we observe them as we want to.*"

In simple words, a paradigm is the way we perceive things. It shapes the way we are all influenced by anything and how we interact with the world. It influences our thought process, actions, and decision-making process. Paradigms are like mental maps that guide us in understanding complex concepts and phenomena because a paradigm is the way of thinking and taking action. It serves as lenses through which we interpret reality. It is not merely related to science, it is correlated to the teenagers' social life as well. To reap better results and productivity, teenagers need to alter their thought process. To alter their thought process, they must **reprogram their brain.** But a question arises, how to do so?

9.2 WAYS TO REPROGRAM YOUR BRAIN

1. Personalization: Teenagers are immensely impacted by their environment. There are pre-existing patterns of thinking that are set in the subconscious mind of a teenager by their environment. These pre-assumptions are not set by their own reasoning.

   For example: Teenagers might believe success means getting an 'A' grade. Because, their environment values academic achievement. Environment enforces the education, it burdens teenagers with getting 'A' grades. However, environment doesn't make them realize the value of education, when realization is needed. Environment makes the realization of value of education when situations go worse. Getting 'A' grade will not be a burden when teenagers realize the value of the grades. Realization is always made when time passes. From an early-stage, it is essential to realize that why education is important? How does it frame teenagers' lives? When teenagers realize the importance, it gets too late. From the early stage teenagers have never considered why it is important? Rather than getting burdened, teenagers can **reprogram their brain and ask themselves: Why is this important?**

As earlier discussed, the environment burdens you with education but doesn't make you realize its importance at the right time. You need to be aware of what's going on in your surroundings. If your environment is enforcing you to pursue something, you can personalize the situation and ask yourself two questions to get a clear idea. The questions:

→ **Why is this important?**

→ **What is the benefit of this in the future?**

2. Filling the voids: It is often seen that when teenagers feel hurdle in overcoming the strenuous situations, they try to put off the situations. They try to delay and put the work off until the next day to overcome the anxiety. Teenagers are aware about that delaying is never the solution but they are still afraid to face it.

   For example: Emma was sitting at her study table, repeatedly staring at email draft on her laptop, which she had to send to her professor. She was trembling with nervousness. She had to deliver this presentation at an upcoming seminar. However, her fingers were twitching and freezing over the keyboard. She had been putting it off for two weeks, convincing herself that she needed more time to work on it. In reality, it was Emma's fear, the fear of failure. She was afraid to present her thoughts in front of a crowd, pondering if her presentation would meet the required expectations. In fact, this wasn't the first time she had delayed something important for a long time. Even before that, she had done the same—avoided, delayed her work and hoped the problem would disappear. One evening, her mother, noticing her unease, sat beside her and asked gently, "What's wrong?" Emma admitted her fear. Her mother listened to her carefully and said, "Emma, if you keep putting off important tasks like this, it will be a hindrance in your personality development. A void will form inside you, filled with regret. It (void) can be filled if you take action. Identify the loopholes that resist you. Explore and fill those voids." That night, Emma opened her diary and scribbled about the fear she had confronted while sending the draft. Then, she prepared a list of small achievable steps to tackle her fear and a list of topics she wanted to improve in the draft. In the end, she wrote a thoughtful reminder for herself: **every time you run, you leave a void behind.** Instead of sending her email immediately, she decided to review the draft. She analysed the draft and made all the required alterations to the presentation. After making the necessary modifications and without thinking about the results, she sent the draft to her professor. Her professor responded enthusiastically, praising her work and encouraging her to present it at the seminar.

This is how Emma analyzed and filled all the voids that had been holding her back.

And also she had reprogrammed her brain to alter the thinking process to resolve the situation.

Teens **need to reprogram their brain by questioning**: What are the voids?

If you feel perplexed, ultimately, you can ask yourself two questions to gain a clarity. The questions:

→ **Where are the voids?**

→ **How can I fill those voids?**

Before filling the voids your brain was thinking in a different way, but since you have filled the voids, your brain has adopted a different perspective which reflects the reprogramming of your brain.

3. Emotional Intelligence: Teenagers are immensely impacted by their emotional wellbeing. Believe it or not, this is true. Emotions cloud thinking abilities. Usually, teenagers make decisions while they lack emotional intelligence.

You can ask yourself two questions. The questions:

→ **Am I making this decision based on how I feel right now**

→ **Is there a need to reconsider the decision?**

"Avoid making any decisions while you are emotionally unstable."

9.3 PHASES OF PRADIGM

Whenever a strenuous predicament occurs, teenagers confront two phases. The phase I reflects the way they solve the situation. The phase II reflects the mindset.

Phase I: It is often seen that when teenagers have to confront some difficult situations. They try to overcome by using the pre-stored information they have. They restrict their thinking abilities. They just use the information they have, to solve the situation and achieve a success. However, when they fail, they feel frustrated. Then they question themselves:

Question: *Why do I have to confront the failures?*

Reason: Teenagers do not analyse the situation properly. They use the pre-stored information to solve the problem.

Solution: They have to alter the way they think. The nature of every situation is distinct. No one can reap results by analysing each situation through a similar approach. It is better to alter the way they ponder. They need to reprogram their brain. For reprogramming their brain, they can follow:

- Personalization
- Filling the voids
- Emotional Intelligence

Apparently, if teenagers alter the way they ponder and analyse the situation, they can fetch better consequences.

Phase II: When teenagers complete the work, they merely set two mindsets:

Mindset-A: I might succeed.

Mindset-B: I might fail.

The perception they set, they limit themselves up to that only. They eliminate the thought of improvement. No matter whether they succeed or fail, they need to focus **whether they improved themselves or not.**

As stated earlier, a paradigm is nothing but, the way we perceive things. To see improvement in yourself, you need to alter your paradigm. You are not short of knowledge; you are short of behavioural patterns. Just change your behavioural patterns.

9.4 HOW DOES PARADIGM SHOWCASES THE UNIQUE WORLD OF A TEENAGER'S LIFE?

Every teenager has their own way of thinking which directly reflects their unique world. The kind of thoughts a teenager has about something directly represents their world. The thinking framework reflects a teenager's world. And when teenagers will alter their framework of thinking, they will showcase their unique world more authentically.

• • •

Key Takeaway: To alter your paradigm, reprogram your brain.

CHAPTER X

Euphoria

10.1 INTRODUCTION

Euphoria is an intense feeling of happiness, often described as an overwhelming sense of joy about things. A teen feels an intense sense of happiness. This might be overlapping with ephemeral gratification, but **euphoria is different from ephemeral gratification. Euphoria refers to a state of intense happiness for the short-term while ephemeral gratification refers to the instant sense of satisfaction or short-term pleasure.** The emotions of elation can peak instantly, which can be referred to as euphoria. The emotions are fleeting in teens.

"Euphoria is just a fleeting moment; true euphoria comes when you feel inner peace and contentment."

The ordinary happiness is rooted in the everyday experiences; however, the euphoria is the feeling of elation which is almost otherworldly. It can be triggered at any moment through various factors.

10.2 WHAT YOU ENJOY?

The significant thing is to find what makes you feel truly happy. To understand what makes you feel more enjoyable, you can follow the below list:

- List all the activities that make you feel elated for a longer time. Remember these activities should not merely give you short-time happiness.
- It is also important to note why these activities are significant for you, if the listed activities are your passion, you are more likely to continue them for a long time.

- It is more obvious that the activities make you feel elated, those things make you feel more connected with yourself.
- Power of Passion: Your passion will have a great impact on your life. If you engage in the activities that you are passionate about it can trigger feelings of euphoria. Whether it's art, learning skills, playing sports, they will help you in your well-being.

10.3 DOES TRUE HAPPINESS EXIST?

Happiness and Euphoria both are distinct. Happiness refers to the long-term contentment on the other hand, euphoria refers to the short-term content. As a teenager, it is important to understand the difference between euphoria and happiness to manage your expectations. Elation is directly linked to expectations.

- If you are more elated you expect more.
- And, if you are less elated you expect less.

How you expect

- Henceforth, when you are in euphoria, you expect more.
- On the other hand, when you feel happiness, you expect less. What does that mean?
  The level of your satisfaction matters a lot. If you are overwhelmed with your desires all the time, then it is obvious that you will be more obsessed with the expectations.

You need to understand that even if you are rejected or get something less than expected, you need to be satisfied with whatever you have. This may sound more philosophical, but this is important if you want to manage your expectations. You need to be satisfied so as not to feel overwhelmed by your desires. Desires lead to presumption. To excel, you need to have patience.

"Patience is hard, but it is the key to achieving results."

10.4 YOUR ULTIMATUM

(Scene: Watson, a 17-year-old teen, approaches a philosopher sitting under a tree, seeking his advice on his struggles.)

Watson: "Wise man, can I ask you something?"

Philosopher: smiled in a way of responding yes to him

Watson: I feel like I am drowning in my dreams. I want to achieve so much—scale up in sports, want to get 'A' grades, start a side business to manage my expenses. I try hard, but no matter how hard I try, it feels like nothing works out for me and I am failing at everything.

Philosopher: (smiled) Ah, the energy of youth—boon and bane. Okay, tell me, young man, do you know what a river teaches us?

Watson: A river? I am not quite sure...

Philosopher: A river reaches its destination by flowing a defined path. It flows in a defined path; if it meanders its path—spreads itself thin it becomes a swamp. However, with boundaries, it carves valleys.

Watson: (Knitting his brows) Do I need to limit my dreams?

Philosopher: Not at all. You must set an ultimatum. No need to restrict your dreams. Just channel your energy effectively. Do you know what matters most to you?

Watson: (articulating with acute insights) My studies and basketball.

Philosopher: Then focus there. Prioritize, plan, take small steps, and evaluate. The rest will follow when the time is right.

Watson: But doesn't it seem like giving up on other dreams like admitting my failure?

Philosopher: Setting boundaries and doing small things does not mean failure.

Watson: Rightly said, wise man. By focusing, I can make real progress instead of feeling lost. Thank you for showing a path.

Philosopher: Follow the path of your purpose. Your river has just begun its journey.

Ultimatum refers to the definite decision or the boundaries you set for yourself. As you experience euphoria daily for your well-being, **it is essential that you know that to what extent you should limit yourself.** This statement neither means that you need to limit yourself nor you need to stagnate your boundary of thinking. Upon seeing this statement, if you thought these two above statements or you have understood that statement merely in the negative aspect then it is crucial to broaden your views. You can even take this statement in the positive aspect wherein you can understand it as: **if I limit my expectations then I can think better, make a realistic plan and can take actions for my targets. This means your limits should be limiting your expectations and become a more realistic individual.** Your ultimatum can not just be limiting your yourself it should also include to think positive about the things. An important benefit of setting your ultimatum is that you can align with your core values and can make a proper decision even in moments of euphoria.

"Your ultimatum will help to grow in true means."

10.5 HOW TO ACHIEVE?

Is it easy to achieve everything in your life? But it might not sound good to the ears if I say—it is complicated to achieve everything. When you set a target in your life, as a teenager, you might aim to crack any competitive exam. You start preparing for that, you work hard for it, and you are scoring good marks in that. You will be over the moon and feel euphoric. You think, "now I will be able to crack the exam." Euphoria falls you into the trap of over-expectation. And, once you fall into the trap of over-expectation, it would ruin your results. It is not bad to think about what you can do after cracking your exam. But as earlier said, you need to avoid over-expectations. To achieve something, you need to have the patience. Get elated over your achievement like scoring good marks, but do not think a lot of about it. You might feel burnout or disappointed due to euphoria. Here is how:

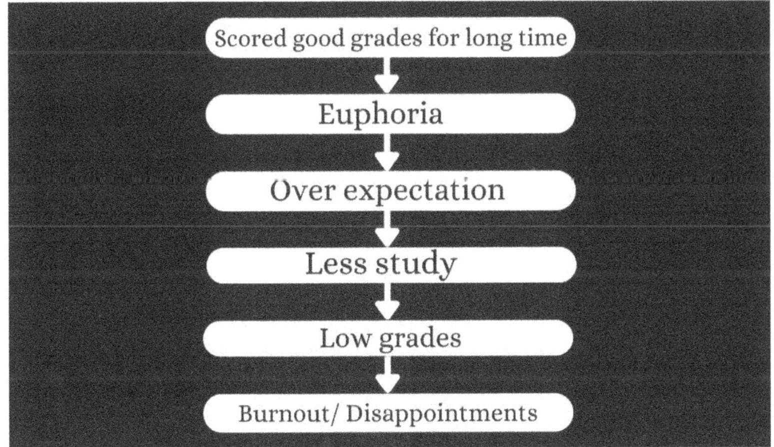

Burnout

Now the question arises: How to achieve anything?

- To achieve anything do not persist euphoria. It sounds contradictory, but it is not. **You can enjoy euphoria, but without over-expectations.** You need to enjoy even the mite moments of your life to feel satisfied with whatever you are doing. Your satisfaction is directly proportional to the continuity of your actions.
Satisfaction ∝ Continuity of your actions

An important thing one must not forget is that life is uncertain, due to which outcome of your input is again really uncertain. Even due to this reason, refrain expecting a lot from your life. Instead, focus on making your 'today' productive as much as you can.

10.6 STABBING IN THE DARK?

When you are in euphoria, you try to stab in the dark. Stabbing in the dark refers to taking risks or making decisions without knowing the consequences. It is like a hit and trial method. This is a common experience, because your emotions got heightened by the intensity of euphoria and you may feel empowered to take risks, believing that the excitement will lead to success. Euphoria creates an illusion that encourages you to take potential risks, making it harder for you to decide whether your decision is truly a profit generator for you or not. As it is alike hit and trail, you never know either it is profitable or not. Stabbing in the dark might lead to growth. Although it is a highly risky process, still taking risk is an essential part of discovering who you are and what you're capable of. How can you avoid stabbing in the dark?

It is not advisable to completely resist stabbing in the dark. To grow in life, taking risks is necessary. One needs to maintain the balance between euphoria and stabbing in the dark. How can one balance this?

There are not any hard and fast rules for this. In euphoria you should not immediately make a decision. Yes, do feel elated if you have achieved something. Even if you need to take risks to grow more, take it! But not instantly. Initially, analyse the consequences as much as you can. Your future is not in your hands, you do not know how it can turn out. If you are aware of the consequences, then you will be able to reduce the number of negative outcomes occurring because of risks.

So, Euphoria is necessary to appreciate every moment of life. If you manage wisely, euphoria will act as a catalyst for your growth, and it will allow you to explore new paths and possibilities without losing sight of what truly matters.

Self-Note

CHAPTER XI

Friendship

Alex and William are sitting on a park bench after school, chatting.

Alex: Hey, William. Can I ask you something?

William: Sure, what's up?

Alex: Who's your best friend?

(William pauses, thinking for a moment.)

William: Well, I'd say it's Oliver, but... lately, I have been feeling like he is a bit green-eyed towards me. I scored higher grades than he did, and it feels like things have changed between us.

Alex: Hmm, maybe you need to rethink that. Friendship shouldn't feel like competition.

William: Indeed, I do need to rethink. It's been on my mind.

Alex: Maybe George? He's cool, but...you know, he tends to gossip a lot.

(Alex pauses for a second, lost in thought.)

Alex: Actually, I have a long list of companions. I just need to think about who's really my best mate.

William: If you've got so many friends, why do you need to think so hard?

Alex: Maybe because... I don't have a best friend at all.

William: Don't stress about it, Alex. Just take your time. You'll figure it out. Anyway, I've got to run. We'll catch up soon?

Alex: Sure, see you later.

(William leaves, while Alex remains seated, lost in thought.)

(For the next few days, Alex couldn't shake the question: "Who is my best friend?" He thought back, tried to figure it out, and scribbled something—A true friend isn't jealous, doesn't share my secrets or mistakes with others... He wondered if such a friend truly existed for him.)

Friendship is considered a vital aspect of teenage life. Friendship plays a role in forming teens' social skills. During this transformative phase, as teenagers venture out to understand the world, they meet various people. It is not apparent to anyone what is the nature of the various people, who they are, what they think or how they react. Teenagers feel closer with peers who share analogous interests, hobbies, and experiences. Friendship can be intense and dynamic.

Friendship may also represent a time period of exploration and building connections. Teenagers easily become friends with alike people due to their camaraderie; however, forming connections for self-growth is dissimilar from making friends. Friendliness is fluid, with new people entering and leaving. An amicable bond is fragile because intense situations can arise at any time. Then the question arises: What does true friendship look like?

- One that is non-fragile, will develop and foster understanding and empathy.
- A true amicable bond will lack envy.
- Your confidential information will be closely guarded.

However, a constant definition of friendship is elusive. As teenagers develop, their friendliness becomes a crucial aspect of emotional support. Having trusted friends helps them navigate the ups and downs of teenage life, providing a buffer against loneliness and isolation. On the other hand, a question arises:

Are all friendships and friends truly authentic?

Giving a direct answer of "yes" or "no" to this question is not justified. As earlier stated, an ideal friendship is one that is non-fragile and offers the emotions of understanding and empathy. There is only a single bond that exists which fulfils requirements of an ideal friendship; that bond is with "parents." Only parents can heal the wounds and provide support under any circumstances. They will be the only ones that would not be envious of your accomplishments. Earlier, it was mentioned that there is no precise definition of amiability; however, parents embody the clearest representation of this concept.

CHAPTER XII

Sui Generis

12.1 INTRODUCTION

'Sui Generis' means 'of its own kind' or 'unique.' We will delve into the concept of uniqueness among teenagers. The uniqueness of every teenager helps in shaping them the way they want to be. Their distinctive traits play a crucial role in—shaping their identities, their decisions, and defining their paths. In line with their unique characteristics, they stand out with unwavering confidence. As each individual holds an unique entity, during adolescence the journey to self-discovery* becomes paramount. It's a time when the pressure to conformity (as discussed in the chapter-8) is immense, yet the desire to stand out carries equal significance. A teenager strongly supports themselves to stand out in the society. This chapter explores how teenagers can embrace their uniqueness while navigating the challenges and opportunities that come in their life journey. You might overlap sui generis with paradigm. However, sui generis is distinct from paradigm. Sui generis emphasizes **uniqueness and individuality,** while a paradigm refers to pattern of **unique thought process,** or belief.

12.2 STAND OUT

Do you know how to know your real worth?

For every teenager, standing out does not necessarily mean being the loudest or the most visible person in society. It's about *identifying and embracing* what makes you different. This could be your passion, your talent, or even your way of thinking. Generally, it refers to something that is unique or in a category of its own, like each teenager's experience.

It is a challenge as well as a triumph to stand out in a world that promotes and prefers conformity. If someone wants to be a notable personality they have to face their own set of challenges, such as facing criticism or feeling isolated. Feeling isolated is not a challenge but rather an opportunity. However, due to the digital world, teenagers feel stressed if they do not have anyone to talk to. The reality of having someone is partially true, because even if you have a friend to talk to but it is not guaranteed that it will be honest to you forever. Being isolated is the best experience since you will learn about yourself. This does not mean that one should avoid socialization. Teenagers should engage in socialization and networking, but they should not share everything with their trusted individuals because no one knows exactly what is in the mind of their trusted individuals. One should allocate time for self-analysis. The knowledge of how to use time adequately in the digital world is essential. One should not merely put their time in one category such as socialization or networking or self-analysis. *It is essential to have adequate knowledge* about the effective use of time. *You have to learn the art of dedicating time to each category:*

- Deadline adherence: completing targets on time
- Networking development: time for building networking
- Introspective time: time for self-analysis

By working on each of these categories, you can realize your true worth. There is not any hard and fast rule to know your worth. When you spend time on each of these categories, you will discover your capabilities and you'll discover your real worth.
These three categories are essential to help you stand out in society. If you keep working, it will help you to achieve your long-term goals. If you don't pursue them, give it a try—you will see improvement in yourself.

"When you self analyse you understand yourself, and also realize your true self—that is when you truly stand out."

12.3 YOU UNIQUE
An important factor in standing out in society is uniqueness; by embracing your uniqueness, you can truly distinguish yourself. It

is obvious that you are distinct based on appearance or voice; however, you should be unique with respect to your *thoughts, notions and habits*. Here is an interesting fact: 'Everyone is unique, and yes! you are unique too.' As you understand your unique character, it will help you in self-acceptance and growth. This will encourage teenagers to reflect on their individuality—what makes them realize who they are. A person can survive with the liabilities, but to live the life utmost, you need assets. Here assets do not correspond to wealth or property. No doubt, wealth is essential, but it is limited. The true asset is your knowledge, your self-realization and your own worth. One should always chase unlimited goods; one example of such a good is knowledge.

Do you know, how to embrace your uniqueness?

You don't have to get external validations to embrace your uniqueness. Your unique passion is unique to you. A practical approach is to ask yourself a question:

How do I feel about this?

As a writer, if you have written something, ask yourself: How do I feel about this?

As a painter, if you have painted something, ask: How do I feel about this?

This question leads to a reflection on various aspects such as:

Am I missing something?

How can I fill the voids?

How can I make this satisfactory?

That is the simple way to embrace your uniqueness because you aren't becoming a pleasure seeker; instead you are validating your work on your own.

12.5 YOUR ASSETS

Everyone has an intrinsic unique trait which can help teenagers conquer the world. When teenagers realize their unique trait, it becomes their assets. Your unique trait could be:

- Digital Skills: mastering programming languages; social media marketing; content creation etc
- Physical Skills: proficiency in sports or athletics; martial arts; fitness training and bodybuilding
- Creative Skills: artistic ability (painting, drawing, sculpture); photography or videography.
- Entrepreneurial Skills: business management; marketing and brand building
- Leadership Skills: team management and collaboration; public speaking

However, if they don't recognize their ability to pursue their unique trait, it might become a liability. However, one should not forget that if you have a succeeding factor, you also have a weakness, which might be challenging for you.

12.6 STEP OUT

Once you have confidence in your skills and knowledge, you will instantly feel empowered to step out of your comfort zone and ready to showcase your true self to the world. When you step out of your comfort zone you will face hurdles and challenges in that. You have to confront your biggest fear.

"Your skills will generate most profitable interest for you if you invest in the knowledge."

• • •

Key Takeaways: Work on three categories that will help you to know your worth.

Embrace your uniqueness by asking: How do I feel about this?

Your unique trait is your asset.

While stepping out, you need to face obstacles.

*Self-Discovery will be discussed in detail in Chapter 17

CHAPTER XIII

Solipsism

13.1 INTRODUCTION

Solipsism is the philosophical and psychological idea that suggests **only our thinking is certain, everything else is an illusion.** Other people and their thinking everything seem to be just hazy. It is closely related to teenagers' thinking. It is a situation of intense inward focus or isolation. Sometimes this inward focus goes far beyond the expectation which will make an individual feel that as if their own thoughts and feelings are the only ones that truly matter or exist. The situation is not just about being self centered; it is far more than that. A teen might feel okay being self-centred for short term; however, this will not be fruitful in the long term. It is helpful, but only up to some extent. In the long term, it would lead to solipsistic thinking. They believe that others should think the way they do and believe what they believe.

13.2 SOLIPSISTIC THINKING

At a young age, teens get attracted to those things easily which are harmful in the long term. Even if someone tries to make them understand the harsh effects, they still do not believe in it. They merely believe in what they have thought at the moment they started something. For instance, it is generally seen that teens are getting attracted to substance abuse. When they have started the consumption at that time they might felt 'relaxed.' At that time, they have not thought of the consequences of the consumption. The few seconds of calmness becomes enormous than their physical and mental health. Their this thinking can be referred to as "Solipsistic Thinking." Teens have a strong belief in their solipsistic thinking, in which they do not believe in anything outside of their own thoughts, even if it would be helpful to them. Teenagers' thinking capabilities gradually grows with time when they begin to understand others' viewpoints better. However, at that time it becomes difficult for them to revive what they have lost. Even regret becomes scarier.

13.3 HOW SOLIPSISTIC THINKING IMPACTS A TEENAGER?

- Negative Solipsistic thinking is adverse: As earlier stated, even if someone tries to make teens understand that either what they believe in is wrong or what they are doing (for instance, substance abuse) is wrong, they will not believe it. Anyone who tries to make them understand this, they will treat them as their enemies. Not everyone is capable of following the criteria of becoming true friends or well-wishers. Merely your parents will follow the criteria. You may not believe it right now, but after some time, you will believe it. Even if you have good friends at some point, they will definitely feel jealous of you, which is obvious. Other than your parents, no one think better of you. Unfortunately, during their teenage years, they often believe that their parents are always against them. Parents are not against you; their thoughts are contradictory to your thinking. When parents oppose your wrong things, your solipsistic mindset grows, and you wanted to stay isolated. You believe that no one else could really understand you. *The solipsistic thinking mindset acts as a hindrance in the personal growth.*

- There is one more important thing: if you merely stick to this mindset, it will be strenuous for you to adapt to the changes in your future life. Let's say, without realizing, you have merely survived your adolescence. Surviving means that you have not worked hard to make your future better. You believed in going with the flow. This clearly indicates that you haven't lived your life. Living life means that you have enjoyed it to the fullest but it does not mean just clubbing or anything else. It means that you have worked hard and faced struggles to reach your goals. That is the real joy. Now, back to surviving life; if you have merely survived your teenage years, then in the later stages of your life, you wouldn't be enough resilient to adapt the changes.

- You will not be able to understand yourself properly and utilise your potential.
- You will be negatively impacting both your mental and physical health.
- You will often find yourself in conflicts or arguments, even without any significant reasons.
- Your reasoning and problem-solving skills will not work effectively.
- You create a distorted self-image because you focus solely on yourself, which leads to overthinking and ultimately distorts your self-perception.
- It can even lead to a void of empathy where you will not be able to realize others' emotions.
- Overall, a teen will face stagnation in all aspects of life—emotionally, academically, personal identity, career, creativity, and intellectual stagnation.

If you stick to this mindset, the consequences are unfolding right before your eyes. That is why it is crucial to overcome the mindset of solipsism.

13.4 WAYS TO OVERCOME

The ways which will be discussed here, they will merely focus on the teenager's personality. Because, teenagers create a distorted self-image due to this behaviour.

- To get rid of solipsistic behaviour and mindset, you need to be more practical about whatever you do.
- Introspection: It is one of the most crucial key point to remember: you can't live without knowing your true self. When you know yourself, your goals, and your aspirations, it becomes strenuous to get distracted. If you still get procrastinated then it indicates that your goals are not clear to you or you might not have interest in that. It is easier to get distracted when your targets are partially clear. It is scientifically proven that you can do anything for a long time if you are passionate about it. I

am interested in Economics, I am keen on understanding how economies work. I can effortlessly study economics even for the whole day. You need to find out. No one can tell you in which thing you are interested, you are the only person who lives with yourself forever. There is a thing: even if you stay with yourself still you don't understand yourself. Isn't that concerning? Although you stay but you don't take efforts to understand your inner self.

- There is an immense need for self-appreciation because you may have already developed a subpar self-image.
- Set a strong mindset to overcome a low self-esteem personality.
- Develop good relations with your parents so that you can share your notions and your problems with them. Generally, it is observed that teenagers are afraid of their parents. There is no need to be afraid of them. Even if you have committed any mistake, do share it with them. They will be the only ones who can help you rectify your mistakes, instead of preaching to others. If you share with them directly, you will be bulwarked.
- Learn your worth and utilise your true potential.
- Define your boundaries so that no one can force you to perform unsuitable task.

Solipsistic thinking can be useful as well, if teenagers believe that their career is the ultimate goal for them. As earlier stated, "solipsistic thinking is about being self-centered." If you prioritize pursuing constructive actions such as living your life (as defined above) you get benefited from that. There is nothing wrong with being this kind of self-centered person. No one, literally no one, can alter the way of teenagers if they are determined. Teenagers do get affected by their environment but to be really honest, it ultimately comes down to you. No matter in how much negative environment you live but literally it is merely up to you.

How do you want to be?

If you wanted to be determined, you would be determined.

On the other hand, if you would incline even once, you would incline forever.

The ultimate thing is, how do you use it?

Choose one

A. To be determined and strong bond with parents.

B. To incline and pursue what others say.

Consequence of choice A: A successful and elated life

Consequence of choice B: An unsuccessful and dreadful life

Choice is yours!

CHAPTER XIV

Cognitive Dissonance

14.1 INTRODUCTION

Cognitive Dissonance is a psychological concept, which refers to the mental discomfort due to an individual's contradictory beliefs and actions. When teenagers hold more than two beliefs and take different actions, they may feel perplexed in selecting what is right to do and what is not. It leads to the creation of internal conflicts and also hinders personal growth. The contradiction in their beliefs and actions leads to stagnate their development. The question is: how to deal with it? We will explore this later.

14.2 FACTORS AFFECTING COGNITIVE DISSONANCE

Nowadays, teenagers fall into the cycle of dissonance—fighting an inner battle between their thoughts and actions. A question might arise: what are the factors contributing to this?

- Social pressure
- Moral conflicts: Teenage is the time period of moral development where, due to abnormal circumstances, they perform unethical actions. It is often seen due to academic pressure, teenagers cheat in their exams. It is not justified to say that they cheated just because they were under pressure. If something is morally wrong, then it should be admitted that it is wrong. That is where they feel dissonance, their morals trying to interpret to them, that what they have done is wrong. What can you do to overcome this? It will be discussed later.
- Desire for social acceptance: They might participate in bullying behaviour to fit into a social group, leading to inner conflict between their actions and values or beliefs.
- Low self-determination: Teens are not merely impacted by their environment. Their thoughts matter a lot. If teenagers are determined towards exactly what they want to pursue, no one

can force them to do something against their will. When you will move to any new place people will force you compulsively either to be like them, or do what they do. However, if you are determined what are your boundaries, what you want to do, no can insist you. On the other hand, if you will incline a little toward their thoughts, they will be able to comply you to be like them and you will fall into the loophole where you have to **fight an inner battle in between your ethics and your actions.**

All the factors are already known, and they are mundane. Even if they are mundane, however, their existence is impacting negatively. A teenager feels so associated and contacted with these factors. No matter how much they avoid them (factors), they still get attracted to them. And that is the reason it becomes crucial to mention these factors.

14.3 CONSEQUENCES

You don't get merely impacted by everything you are surrounded by. What you do and what you believe in, are often distinct during adolescence. If so, then the consequences will not be fruitful. *Your actions must get align with your beliefs and so do your beliefs must get aligned with your actions.*

- **Ineffectiveness in the work**: Alex is a 16-year-old high school student who believes that studying hard is key to achieving his dream of becoming a doctor. However, after school each day, instead of reviewing his notes or hitting the books, he spends hours scrolling through social media, watching videos, and chatting with friends. This creates a conflict for him: he values education and wants to succeed, but on the other hand, his daily habits do not reflect that belief. As a result, his test scores are lower than he hoped, leaving him feeling ineffective and frustrated with his efforts. Although he knows that he needs to change his routine, still he struggles to resist distractions, which leads to a decline in his academic performance. In the end, the consequence is *ineffectiveness in his work.*

- **Anxiety:** Sophie is a 15-year-old aspiring athlete who always believes that living a healthy lifestyle is essential for her success. She follows her strict training and diet planning. However, when she is with her friends, she often feels pressured to fit in and ends up indulging in junk food, sugary snacks and hight-fat food. While she reassures herself that it is merely a one-time treat, these moments happen more often than she would like to admit. Each time she deviates from her disciplined routine, she feels increasingly anxious. After indulging, she can't shake off the worry that it might negatively impact her athletic progress. Despite her strong belief in consuming healthy meals, but the conflict between her actions and her beliefs leads to anxiety.
- **Self-Doubt:** Lily is a talented artist who believes that creativity is a vital part of her identity. She dreams of displaying her artwork in a local gallery and gaining recognition for her skills. However, after finishing each piece, she is often hit with intense self-doubt. "What if no one likes it?" she worries. Even though she believes in her talent, she struggles to share her work, afraid of what others might think. One day, her art teacher encourages her to submit a piece for a school exhibition. At first, Lily is excited about the chance to showcase her art. But as she starts to prepare her submission, her self-doubt returns. She begins comparing her work to her classmates', thinking, "Their art is so much better than mine. What if I embarrass myself?" Despite knowing she has talent, she considers pulling out altogether, feeling like she doesn't deserve a spot in the exhibition. If she had believed in herself, she might have received a positive response. Even if a single person had appreciated her efforts, that would motivate her. Due to her internal conflicts, she ended up losing a good opportunity from her hands.
- **Dilemma:** Emma cares a lot about the environment and highly believes in protecting plants at all costs. She is an active member of her school's sustainability club, where she encourages recycling, reusing and saving energy. However, she faces a dilemma when her best friend invites her to go shopping at a

fast-fashion store known for harming the environment. Emma feels stuck between wanting to stick to her beliefs and worrying about disappointing her best friend. She wants to join in on the fun with her friends, but shopping at a store that goes against her values makes her feel conflicted. What can Emma do now? This will be discussed later.

- **Stagnant Self-Growth:** Ethan is a 17-year-old who believes in the importance of lifelong learning and self-improvement. He often talks about how stepping out of his comfort zone can help him develop new skills and expand his horizons. However, despite his strong beliefs, he finds himself stuck in a routine. He goes to school, plays video games with his friends, and spends his weekends doing the same things. One day, Ethan's school announces a robotics club, which catches his interest. He has always been fascinated by technology and coding, and he thinks this could be a great chance to learn something new. However, when he considers joining the club, self-doubt creeps in. "What if I'm not good enough?" he worries. "What if I can't keep up with everyone else?" Instead of getting rid of his fears and he avoided to attend the first meeting, he convinces himself to wait until next semester when he feels more ready. As the months go by, Ethan continues to avoid joining the club. Meanwhile, his friends participated in the club, learned new skills as well as gained confidence. However, Ethan remains stuck in his comfort zone which clearly indicates stagnation in his growth. His thoughts resisted him to take actions.

As you have seen in each case, the thoughts and believes were not aligning with each other. Similarly, if your beliefs and actions don't align with each other, you will inevitably have to face negative consequences.

14.4 WAYS TO AVOID DISSONANCE

Cognitive Dissonance is nothing but the conflict in your mind between your thoughts, more precisely your **morals, and in your actions**. Your persuasions and your actions are the foundational blocks; if they are aligned, your mind would be free from all sorts of inner battle.

- **Alter your actions:** As we discussed in the moral conflicts, your morals were different from your actions. (Your morals: not to cheat; your action: cheating.) What should you do now? Do you need to change your perception? Not at all, you don't have to alter your morals. Your actions should be altered here. Your action should be to study. To avoid your inner battle, emphasize yourself to take actions.

- **Alter your Persuasions:** As we discussed in the Dilemma, Emma has to choose either to align with her thoughts and refrain from enjoyment or to go with her friends and enjoy. The environment is a greater concern, Emma can either change her persuasion or her action. She wanted to go shopping with her friends but without altering her belief. She can make her friends understand the harmful impacts made by the store and persuade them to go to another store. This way by staying connected with her belief she was also able to perform her action (going to the store and enjoying.) She managed to hit two birds with one stone. She made her friends understand about the importance of the environment and she even enjoyed with her friends. **She transformed the idea of mere enjoyment into a productive act of persuasion** *(changed her friend's belief.) She was able to align with her beliefs. Her beliefs got protected and also, she was able to carry out the action (enjoyment.)*

The coordination between beliefs and actions is vital. As earlier stated, "The contradiction between beliefs and actions leads to stagnation in personal development." To overcome this, one needs to balance their beliefs and actions. Your persuasions and actions play a crucial role In almost every aspect of your life.

- Your positive persuasions and positive actions will suppress negative persuasions and negative actions.

Positive persuasion	Strong determination and persistence
Positive action	learning any new skill: ABC
Negative persuasion	Let's us do it later!
Negative action	Scrolling or chatting

Persuasions and actions

Fill this, to understand what are your persuasions and actions.

Positive persuasion	
Positive action	
Negative persuasion	
Negative action	

Your persuasions and actions

Note: You can fill this, to track that what you belief in and what you are pursuing. It can serve as a real-time tracker to help you understand what you're doing versus what you believe. Create a sticky note of this, paste it wherever you find it convenient, so you can stay aligned with your beliefs and actions.

CHAPTER XV

Enhancement

We shape ourselves and our thoughts help us alter our perspectives. When we embark on a new endeavor, we feel excited. But, after a few days of working on it, we experience some prominent feelings such as feeling anxious, a lack of authenticity and diminished self-confidence. We are uncertain whether it is right for us or not! Still, we do.

When you enter a new educational institution—whether it is a school, college, university or enrolling yourself in skill courses to learn something new. The steps you take to enter the institution do not merely resemble your physical steps; they represent your ambitions, your visions, your persistence and your determination. You enter with a wider and broad perspective, not only to enhance your life, but also to enhance yourselves. **Enhancement in life and enhancement in oneself,** both are distinct. Enhancing your life can be defined as *enhancement in the long run* and enhancement in oneself can be referred to as the *improvement of yourselves on a daily basis.* Your perspective and vision can never be limited. When you enter, you take your steps with a vision of making wholesome efforts you want to put into academic and other extracurricular activities.

When you think about enhancing your life, it will be a protracted process. It requires fostering habits. Your habits will merely help you in becoming inexorable. It is strenuous to overcome any negative habit, but if you want to pursue any task or work for a longer time and stay consistent, then it will be helpful to prioritize that task as your top priority with assiduous effort. When you perform the task immutably and by emphasizing quality over quantity, it will become your positive habit. To reap out better from life, it is necessary to have habits and your major focused habits will be helpful for you to enhance in the life. There is a saying: "Rome wasn't built in a day." Similarly, no one can be a good writer in a day. A good reader makes reading a habit, a good sportsperson practices daily, a good speaker has the habit of speaking daily. These tasks are helpful in long run and these tasks can be considered as enhancement in life.

Just as habits are required in the long run for life enhancement, similarly, enhancing oneself requires working daily to develop positive habits.

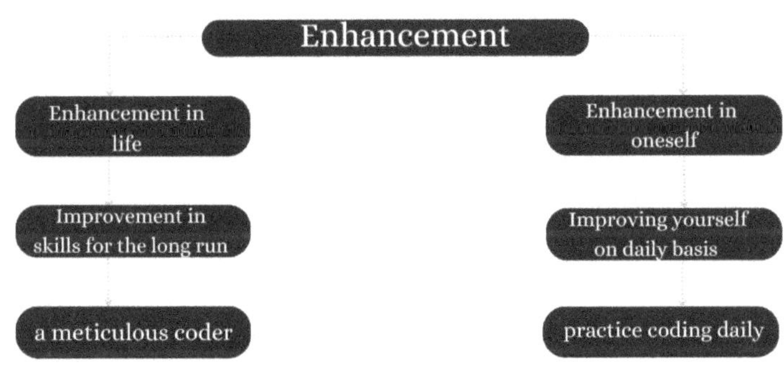

Enhancement

Now, the question arises: What is meant by a broader vision?
A broader vision does not mean merely achieving academic scores; learning new skills is essential. Teenagers feel more mature, resilient, and capable of facing challenges when they gain experience in distinct fields as skills are not limited to any particular field. When teenagers move out of their sheltered boundaries for commencement of their journey, that is where skills become a prerequisite and a broader vision plays a significant role there.

CHAPTER XVI

Overcoming Adversity (Quotes)

72

"When mountains break, stones are created—each one a living hope. With the effort of accumulating these stones, the mountains can be rebuilt. Similarly, in times of adversity, create a hope to rebuilt yourself by aggregating your strengths."

73

"Adversity shapes us; it builds our resilient character for tomorrow."

74

"There is no need to overthink to overcome adversity; it is just like a test which is examining your determination towards your goal."

CHAPTER XVII

Self-Discovery

When teenagers reach adolescence, they begin their journey by exploring themselves, distinct niches, beliefs, passions, hobbies, notions and individuality. When the exploration period begins, they start questioning societal norms and expectations. However, teenagers primarily focus on understanding their own values. Teenagers start scouting and engaging in different activities such as arts, sports, social groups, experimenting with distinct roles and following diverse hobbies. All these activities help teenagers to engage in various fields, giving them opportunities to venture more and socializing. These kinds of activities play an important role in demonstrating the strengths and weaknesses of an individual. "Exploring" and "engaging" help in analysing the individuality. A teenager is able to discover himself. But one question arises:

What does 'discovering oneself' mean?

In simpler words, it can be stated as exploring oneself.

Nevertheless, the term **'discovering oneself' cannot be limited to simply–exploring oneself.**

Discovering is about venturing into the attainable domains, immersing in the distinct domains to identify strengths and weaknesses. When you master one skill you can't limit yourself up to that merely, keep on exploring more domains because if you limit yourself, your growth will be halted and you will be stagnant. When an individual follows this process, it can be considered as the "Self-Discovery." It is a transformative journey, where teenagers ask themselves and explore their identities across various fields. Self-discovery is the process of understanding one's values. When a child enters adolescence, the process of self-discovery begins. But what does self-discovery include?

Self-discovery includes contemplating one's emotions, desires, and fears. Self-discovery may be related to introspection, but introspection is the examination or observation of one's own mental and emotional processes, while self-discovery is the exploration of ourselves in distinct domains. The introspective process is a dissimilar process.

The process of self-discovery can be confusing as well, as the challenges during exploration are uncertain. Every challenge comes with its own sort of opportunity; so both opportunities and challenges are helpful for self-growth. During this process, teenagers learn to distinguish between societal expectations and their authentic desires. They challenge limiting beliefs, *accept their imperfections* and learn to embrace their uniqueness through self-challenge. Self-challenge and Self-discovery work in parallel but both work effectively for personal transformation. A teenager can 'Self-challenge' to do 'Self-discovery.'

It serves as a key factor in identifying personal passions and career interests. This newfound purpose helps in developing un-hazy meaning of life as they explore their interests and values and also serves as a guiding force in their decision-making and goal-setting.

"You grow as you explore yourself and your surroundings."

A teenager who has already explored himself and his passions during his teenage will feel more confident, less stressed and will embrace his uniqueness. He will have the spirit of inner peace and contentment. The process of self-discovery helps him appreciate the people around him. Under stress a teen cannot even embrace itself, then it is certain that how could a teenager appreciate others. Teenagers perceive hidden strengths. The journey of self-discovery is of *self-compassion,* which allows teenagers to be kind to themselves as they navigate the complexities of their identities. The process of self-discovery is not limited to a specific age; it is an ongoing journey that continues even into adulthood.

CHAPTER XVIII

Finding your Voice

What is finding your voice?
When teenagers understand their individuality, it can be considered that they have found their voice.
What does individuality mean? And is it similar to self-discovery?
Finding your voice is distinct from self-discovery. Self-discovery is about venturing across the attainable domains, immersing in the distinct domains to know the strengths and weaknesses while finding your voice is about self-awareness and introspection.

Finding your voice has two inevitable factors which are self-awareness and introspection. Discovering your self-directed thoughts, opinions, notions and perspectives is essential for finding your voice which allow teenagers to **assert their individuality and contribute to meaningful conversations.** Your **individuality** is measured on the basis of your self-directed notions, creativity and ways to deal with situations which are merely unique to you. Expressing oneself in society is crucial for every teenager. Individuality helps teenagers stand out in the community which represents their unique characteristics.

Introspection involves observation of one's own mental health and emotional processes. Often teenagers reflect on their experiences, emotions, and thoughts to uncover what truly matters to them. This reflection is helpful for a teenager to understand the one's capabilities, inner motivation level, how resilient they are!

Finding your voice helps in evacuating from opulence zone. It allows them to resist conformity and express their authentic selves. It is a process of breaking free from limitations. They gain the confidence to speak up against injustices. Discovering your voice involves overcoming self-distrust and fear of judgment. And it also helps them learn and believe their opinions and insights, even if they differ from others. Finding your Voice can be helpful for teenagers especially influencing in creative pursuits. Activities like art, writing, music, or other forms of expression teenagers learn to channel their thoughts and emotions into their work, leaving a unique mark on the world. As stated earlier, finding your voice helps a teenager stand out and speak with confidence, but it is also about actively listening to others. They learn to appreciate diverse perspectives. The way to find your voice is through self-awareness, but sometimes role models and mentors also help by encouraging them to express themselves authentically. Teens are able to strengthen their voice. They are able to refine their words, encounter new experiences, and build a strong foundation. What are the ways to enrich self-awareness and introspection?

1. Do self-discovery.
2. Work in your interested niche that excites you and make you feel happier.
3. You will realize your potential while working, which will be considered as self-awareness.
4. The way you will handle difficult situations (emotionally, technically, mentally) while working is considered introspection.

Self-awareness	realizing your potential while working
Introspection	the way you handle difficult situations while working: emotionally, mentally and technically

Finding your voice

A person who has strong introspection and self-awareness, that person has found his voice, nevertheless, it cannot be denied that *finding your voice is an ongoing process*. As teenagers find their voice, they become resilient in handling situations, shape their identities and make a positive impact on their communities and on the world.

CHAPTER XIX

Coping with Anxiety and stress

When a teen enters adolescence scrounging with stress becomes a prodigious concern. But it is not only the case for a particular age group; every age group has to stumble. Teenage can be a challenging time, marked by academic pressures, social changes, and self-discovery. Learning effective coping strategies equips teenagers with the tools to manage stressors and navigate the complexities of their lives. They need to recognize the signs of stress and anxiety. It could involve the sleep cycle, mood swings, and physical symptoms. A teen can seek help from their parents, adult siblings or even from trusted mentors or counsellors but only those mentors who can be fully trusted because of the privacy invasion. As discussed earlier in the 'Friendship' chapter share your secrets only with those who will neither unwrap your secrets nor use them as a weapon against you. It becomes hard to share feelings with others, as thoughts are infinite, which creates a perplex to apprehend. As time passes, the thoughts start becoming more intricate; until a teenager wouldn't share with anyone.

This myth can be denied: it is requisite that one must share their thoughts with others.

One can even have a self-talk to avoid feeling adjudicated. It is an individual preference with whom one chooses to share their deliberations. If a teenager wants to share their own deliberations with themselves, then *self-awareness* is the first step in addressing these challenges. Unless one is aware of their behaviour or individuality, it seems complicated to tackle the dilemmas.

And if one wants to share their deliberations with anyone else, one must keep two thoughts in their mind:

- That person knows you and understand you.

- Someone who is incorruptible so that you can have an open conversation without feeling adjudicated and that person does not brutalize the information against you in the future. "There are only two individuals who can be trusted fully in the mournful situations – they are Parents."

Another method to cope with stress is: ***healthy lifestyle habits***, including regular exercise, a balanced diet, and requisite sleep, play a significant role in managing stress and anxiety. Engaging in physical activity helps in promoting a positive mood. Relaxation techniques, such as deep breathing exercises and meditation, can help teenagers to reduce feelings of anxiety. Time management skills are crucial for handling academic and extracurricular activities. Learning to prioritize tasks and break them down into manageable steps plays a significant role. To reduce the stress, it is necessary that a teenager must set realistic goals which are accomplishable. There are two things which one must commemorate:

- *Perfectionism is not obligatory.*
- *Mistakes are opportunities for self-growth.*

Engaging in creative activities, such as art, music, or writing, provides an outlet for self-expression and stress relief. Limiting exposure to excessive screen time can significantly decrease feelings of anxiety.

It is necessary to have someone who can understand you better, guide you and should be trustworthy since it is hard to find someone like this, so it is far better to be a self-companion. One can practice the ***self-companion process***—a process where a teenager can try to understand themselves better, which will include activities such as understanding their own worth, accepting the way as you are, learning to handle yourself even in mournful situation.

It is okay to say 'no' to commitments which make you exhausted. These commitments might include promises you made to friends about going out, but if they are becoming a hindrance to completing your tasks, then simply say no.

Distractions make a teenager frustrated, using various sites for a long time increases the frustration. To refrain from that frustration, it is better to indulge oneself in their areas of interest and preferred niche. Activities aligned with one's self-interest will be quite helpful and because of this, the fear of chaos caused by distractions and resistance in productivity can be minimized, so you don't have to stress about doing projects.

> *"Engage with yourself to avoid the chaos."*

The art of learning to **accept uncertainty** is essential. Practicing gratitude can help shift from negative repercussions to deliberative thinking. Avoid accessing too much data through social-media to be stress free. Healthy communication skills enable teenagers to express their feelings and needs, reducing internalized stress. **Focusing on the present moment** instead of ruminating on the past or worrying about the future can alleviate anxiety. Understanding that **perfectionism is an unrealistic approach.** We tend to strive for perfection, and until one attains it, stress can persist. Therefore, it's better to let go of that stress and focus on improving day by day.

> *"The more stress one experiences, the more addictive it can become."*

A mite amount of stress is helpful as it will remind your brain to complete a specific task such as completing school assignments or projects. Although the consumption of anything is okay up to a certain level only, the excess is always atrocious.

To overcome stress, you can question yourself:

Is this adversity worth stressing over?

"When you reflect on the answer, certainly, half of your stress will naturally dissipate!

CHAPTER XX

Epiphany

20.1 INTRODUCTION

An epiphany is a sudden moment of clarity, insight or profound realization that can change how you see things. It often happens unexpectedly, like a light bulb turning on, and brings a fresh understanding of something that once seemed confusing or out of reach. It can also refer to the sudden realization of your mistakes. The realization can be triggered by an experience, conversation or might be due to self-reflection. You will not learn directly from your experiences; you have to reflect on your actions that caused you trouble. During an epiphany you will observe a shift in your beliefs, goals and actions because you will be realizing the consequences occurred due to your earlier beliefs, goals and actions.

The extensivity to do something leads to harmful impacts. For example, to be an obsessive social media addict. In the obsession of social media, teens usually forget about their privacy. It is usually seen when teens have to confront harmful impacts, only then do they have a sobering epiphany. It is more helpful to learn from others' experiences, a lot of bits of news reported daily regarding data privacy. Ultimately, our safety lies in our hands.

With the help of an epiphany, a teen can realize a new way to approach a problem, or it can be life-changing, prompting one to rethink about their career and beliefs. These moments often encourage growth and inspire you to make positive changes. It can help you break your old habits, behaviour patterns and can offer a sense of direction or purpose you may not have had before. Experiencing an epiphany can empower you to uncover a truth about yourself or the world. It acts as a constant reminder to keep learning and evolving your uniqueness.

20.2 NASCENT

Nascent is closely related to Epiphany. Nascent refers to something that is newly formed, but it grows rapidly. Again, the above example can be taken, as teens get in touch with multiple people over the internet without knowing their real identity and not being concerned about their own privacy, which is not healthy for teens. When epiphany hits, they develop a nascent character, which means when they suddenly realize, they rapidly develop an opposite identity—becoming more concerned about their privacy than before.

20.3 ALIENATION

During the nascent phase, a teen experiences alienation. Alienation refers to isolation from others or even sometimes from oneself. Alienation due to nascent behaviour is harmful to a teen's mental well-being. It will impact a teen socially, mentally, and academically. A teen will face resistance in their growth. On the other hand, if a teen isolates themself in a positive manner, it will be useful for the teen. Positive manner means isolating themselves to learn, develop new skills and work on themselves to grow. This alienation will never disappoint a teen.

Positive Alienation

Emma always wanted to learn coding but with school and hanging out with friends, she could never find the time. So, one summer, she decided to skip her usual plans and spend her days practicing. She cut back on social activities and focused on learning the basics and gradually moved on to the advanced level. At first, it felt strange not being around her friends, but as she got better at coding, she began to feel proud of herself. By the end of the summer, she could design a website. Taking a break from her social life had been worth it—it gave her a new skill and a real sense of achievement.

Negative Alienation

Excessive social media exposure in one's life leads one to forget about their own privacy, which results in detrimental consequences. In the end, a teen has to confront negative alienation.

It is up to the teen to choose:

A. Positive alienation - Personal Growth
B. Negative alienation - Resistance to Growth
Your choice, either A or B

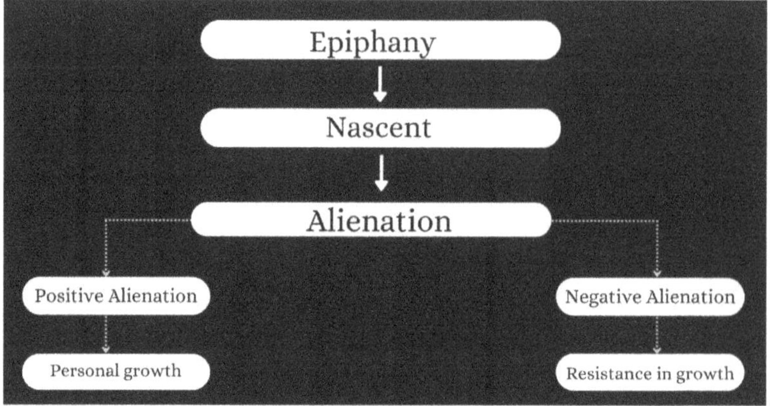

Epiphany Cycle

20.4 DO YOU HAVE TO SOCIALIZE?

Socialization is crucial, but it is all about how you socialize.

It plays a vital role in development. It helps in building your career and expanding your knowledge. When you set up connections with career-oriented people like mentors, industry professionals, and peers, it becomes the key to opening new doors to new opportunities. You gain access to internships, networking events, and group projects—all of which are key for personal and professional growth. Some of the key advantages are:

- By building connections, you can learn from others' experiences and viewpoints which will broaden your perspective on a variety of topics. You will get better understanding of your niche and you will also be able to improve your innovative and critical thinking.
- Your thinking will be enhanced by participating in group projects or attending events that provide hands-on experience,

which is often more impactful than just learning from books.

- You will be enhancing your interpersonal skills and learning about teamwork, both of which are best developed through social interaction. Working with others not only helps you in enhancing skills but also helps in boosting your confidence in professional settings.

In short, socializing is a rewarding experience that fosters growth, adaptability, and success whether in education, career, or life in general.

20.5 APLOMB

To overcome epiphany, you need to have strong aplomb. Aplomb is the ability to handle pressure or difficult moments with grace. If your aplomb is strong, it will be effortless to overcome all vicissitudes. It helps them navigate situations like exam pressure, social conflicts, handle criticism constructively, or public speaking, all with a sense of control, even in high-pressure scenarios.

20.6 HOW TO HANDLE CRITISM

To handle criticism, never look at who criticized you; always focus on the words. It does not matter who said something negative about you. You need to overlook for what you have been criticized for.

- If you are criticized over your physical appearance, there is no need to worry about it. You are a creation of God, and God has made everyone unique. You also have qualities that will make you stand out from others.
- If you are criticized for something you do not know, simply learn it.

Just improve yourself for what you have criticized for. That's a simple rule!

WHILE IMPROVING YOURSELF, JUST CHERISH YOUR PATHWAY.

6 Practical Tips on how to thrive in Life

1.	Tip	Understand and manage your Internal Conflicts. (The internal conflicts are the internal battles which you experience with your own thoughts, emotions and expectations.)
	Method	Self-awareness
	Appro--aches	To know yourself better, apply JQS approach. • J stands for Journaling (write down what you feel) • Q stands for Questioning (Question yourself) • S stands for Self-talk (Talk to yourself in front of the mirror or just record yourself)
2.	Tip	Utilize your maximum energy. (It refers to utilizing your maximum energy as soon as possible to get maximum output.)
	Method	Manage your Time
	Appro--aches	• Utilize your peak energy hours (Try to complete big goals when you wake up instead of just responding to emails.) • Set flexible hours for yourself (No strict planner, plan your day simpler like doing any XYZ task for 2 hours, other ABC task for 1 hour.
3.	Tip	Develop a growth mindset
	Method	Change the way you preceive things.
	Appro--aches	• Reframe your negative thoughts. Instead of saying *I can't do this*; say *I am learning how to do this.* • Appreciate your efforts: Try to celebrate your small wins and also try to appreciate the learning which you have made during the process.

4.	Tip	Handle your failures.
	Method	Choose a different route. Don't constantly think about failures.
	Appro--aches	• Bounce back quickly to your routine: Don't give yourself time to feel disappointed, instead think about what you can do to perform better next time. • Ask yourself: What went wrong? Shift from blaming yourself to learning.
5.	Tip	Building Consistency.
	Method	Create new habits less frictional or easy to do.
	Appro--aches	• Create flexible (easy to do) but rigid (do it consistently) habits. • Remind yourself about your new routine until it becomes your *habit.
6.	Tip	Challenge your self-doubt
	Method	Put it aside by questioning and acting
	Appro--aches	• Ask yourself for evidence. Question yourself: "What proof do I have that I can't do this?" • Take small actions to overcome self-doubt. You can start with a tiny steps such as reading one page or speaking once a week. The actions you will take to overcome the fear it weaken your self-doubt over time.

*In bond with reality of life (first book), I've covered how to turn routine into habits.

NO	TIPS	SIGNIFICANCE
1.	Understand and manage your Internal Conflicts	Help to control the emotions
2.	Utilize your maximum energy	Help to manage the time
3.	Develop a growth mindset	Help to develop the growth mindset
4.	Handle your failures	Help in handling failures
5.	Building Consistency	Help in building distractionless life
6.	Challenge your self-doubt	Help to overcome self-doubt

Short Note For Readers

Dear Readers,

Thank you so much for taking the time to read this book. It has been a pleasure sharing my work with you.

Teenage is a phase of true hustle; life is meant to be lived, not to be survived. If you understand what is exactly teenage is, you can live your life utmost. Before including others in your life just make sure to first indulge yourself in your life. You need to have a conscience of who you are!

Life is more than simply going with the flow—it's about seeking experiences that make you feel alive. Take time to do what makes you happy and explore the world with curiosity and passion.

Knowing your own worth is key to living an authentic life. Your value is not based on what others think. Embrace what makes you unique, appreciate your strengths, and remember that you deserve respect just as you are. Once you recognize your worth, you'll never settle for less than you deserve.

Living in line with your values is essential for finding peace and purpose. Your values act as a guide which will help you make decisions and face challenges with integrity.

Having a healthy bond with your parents will provide a strong foundation in your life. While misunderstandings happen, open communication with parents and respecting them can build trust and deepen your bond.

Building a network is crucial for success in your career. Surround yourself with people who inspire you and open doors to new opportunities.

True happiness lies in doing what you like, achieving your goals, and building meaningful relationship with parents. When you nurture this sense of fulfilment, it can drive you towards a more meaningful, sustainable and satisfactory life.

    With gratitude,

Sukhmanpreet Kaur

As you have made it to the end. I have created a short quiz for you. It is not to judge you, but to help you understand yourself a little better. No overthinking, just answer what feels right.
Scan the QR code and begin.
Let's see what you discover about yourself.

Scan this for free Assessment Quiz

Author Page

Sukhmanpreet Kaur is a passionate writer whose literary journey has been inspired by her mother's unwavering support. She is passionate about sharing her thoughts with the world through her books. Writing has always been more than a hobby for her and she hopes to continue reaching readers everywhere.

According to Sukhman, *Writing is the best companion.* This is the author's third book. She has already written two books, entitled "Bond with the Reality of Life" and "The Effect of Thoughts." At the age of 17, she has published her first two books.

Apart from her solo works, she is also the co-author of four anthologies. She is in 3rd year of her graduation and recently she has published a Punjabi Novel entitled "Banjar Zameen."

(To read the novel, kindly text on this instagram handle: @author_sukhman_dhadde)

CONNECT WITH THE AUTHOR:
Instagram: @author_sukhmanpreet_kaur
YouTube: @author_sukhmanpreet_kaur

or simply scan the QR code to connect with the author.